Overcoming
Procrastination

I've Been Meaning To Write
This Book for Years ...

Chris Ball

www.ChrisBall.com

Chanthology

www.chanthology.com

Paperback Edition: ISBN 978-1-915449-84-9
Hardback Edition: ISBN 978-1-915449-86-3
E-book Edition: ISBN 978-1-915449-85-6

Overcoming Procrastination

I've Been Meaning To Write This Book for Years …

Contents

Introduction

Procrastination is not just about poor time management or laziness; it's a complex behavioural issue that affects many people across various aspects of their lives. Whether delaying starting a project, avoiding financial responsibilities, or even postponing your dreams, procrastination can be a significant barrier to achieving your full potential.

Why do we procrastinate? Often, it's because tasks seem overwhelming, fears become paralysing, or distractions pull us from what we know we need to accomplish. In this book, you will understand the deep-rooted psychological factors behind procrastination and learn practical strategies to combat them effectively. Each chapter is designed to take you step-by-step through understanding, addressing, and finally overcoming procrastination.

Consider the story of Sarah, a graphic designer, who had harboured a dream of running a marathon for as long as she could remember. As marathons rolled through her city each year, she watched the runners with a mixture of admiration and a deep, lingering desire to be with them. Sarah's running shoes collected dust despite her strong aspirations, and her training plans remained just plans. Her procrastination was not born out of laziness but a shadow of doubt that crept in every time she considered starting: What if she couldn't finish? What if she was the last one across the finish line?

This cycle of anticipation and retreat continued for years, with Sarah resetting her "start date" time and again. Each postponed plan compounded her sense of frustration and helplessness, making the starting line seem even further away. She felt stuck, unable to move past the comfort of the familiar routine that required no risk of failure.

As her 30th birthday approached, a stark realisation struck Sarah. The years were slipping by, and her dream was no closer to becoming a reality. It was a now-or-never moment. Determined not to let her fears dictate her life any longer, Sarah took a decisive step: she registered for the upcoming city marathon scheduled six months ahead. This commitment was the external push she needed to transition from intention to action.

Sarah began breaking her large goal into smaller, more manageable daily tasks to confront her procrastination habit. She started with short, consistent runs, no matter the weather or how she felt. No matter how trivial it seemed, each completed run was a victory over her previous self, who would have found an excuse to delay.

Joining a local running club also provided Sarah with the community support she lacked when training alone. With each group run, her confidence surged. She wasn't the fastest, but that no longer mattered. What mattered was showing up, day after day.

The day of the marathon was a cold, clear morning. As Sarah lined up with thousands of others, the nerves were there, but so was an unshakeable sense of achievement. Crossing the finish line, Sarah was not first, nor was she last—but she had finished, and that was all she needed. The marathon was more than a race; it was a physical manifestation of her mental journey.

This breakthrough was transformative for Sarah, proving that the barriers of procrastination can be dismantled with structured goals and consistent action. Her success in the marathon encouraged her to tackle other areas of life with the same strategy, turning dreams into tangible achievements.

This book will serve as both a mirror and a map. It will reflect the many ways procrastination might manifest in your life and provide a clear path forward, filled with actionable steps to reclaim your time and productivity. You will discover how setting small, achievable goals can transform an overwhelming project into an exciting adventure. You will learn to reframe your fears and recalibrate your mindset for success. And importantly, you will discover how to create a sustainable routine that aligns with your personal and professional aspirations.

Whether you're a student struggling to complete assignments on time, a professional buried under a backlog of tasks, or someone who's put off pursuing their passions, this book is for you. It's designed to equip you with the tools you need to manage your tasks and understand and adjust the underlying attitudes and behaviours that contribute to procrastination.

By the end of this book, you won't just be planning to make changes; you'll be in the midst of an exciting new way of living, free from the unnecessary stress and guilt that procrastination brings. Get ready to take control of your time, confidently tackle your tasks, and start moving towards the life you've always wanted.

For years, I harboured a deep-seated desire to write and create books that would inspire and guide others toward achieving their goals and dreams. Yet, a significant personal challenge stood in my way—dyslexia. This learning difficulty made reading and writing a slow and laborious process for me. As I attempted to pen my thoughts, they often slipped away before I could fully articulate them on paper, leaving me with fragments of ideas that never quite blossomed into the stories I envisioned.

The frustrations of my school days, when reading aloud in class was a source of embarrassment and shame, lingered long into adulthood. These experiences left a mark, instilling a persistent fear of failure. The dread of crafting something subpar, something that might evoke ridicule or criticism, was daunting.

This fear was not just about the act of writing itself but about exposing a part of me that I had long viewed as inadequate.

The emotional barriers remained formidable despite technological advances that somewhat levelled the playing field—speech-to-text software for writing and grammar checkers for editing. Over the years, I enthusiastically started numerous book projects, only to see them fizzle out, unfinished. The one time I actually published a book, I pulled it off sale within a few days, succumbing to a compulsive need to rewrite it yet again, driven by a relentless fear of not being "good enough."

Realising that my aspirations would remain unfulfilled unless I confronted these fears head-on, I decided to seek external support. I enlisted a writing coach to provide structure and accountability and a content editor to help refine and polish my manuscripts. These weren't just professional supports; they were my pillars in navigating the emotional turmoil that writing stirred within me.

With their encouragement and a structured approach to my writing schedule, I began dedicating daily time to my craft. Slowly, the pages started to fill with words that felt true to my voice. The more I wrote, the more the fear receded, giving way to a newfound confidence.

Now, as I pen this book, the book I have dedicated years to is in the final stages of editing, and preparations are underway for its publication under the title "Winning The Game." It represents not just a personal victory over the hurdles of dyslexia and fear of failure but also a message to others that with the right support and determination, it is possible to transcend personal limitations and achieve one's dreams.

This journey has taught me that writing, like any profound endeavour, is not just about the end product but about confronting and overcoming the inner obstacles that stand in the way. I hope this book not only serves as a guide to overcoming

Introduction

procrastination but also as an inspiration for anyone facing their fears, reminding them that they are capable of more than they might believe.

Your journey to overcoming procrastination starts here. It's not just about getting things done; it's about understanding why you delay them in the first place and changing your approach to work and life. Let's begin this transformative journey together.

Understanding Procrastination

Welcome to the first chapter of our journey into the depths of procrastination. Procrastination is a familiar foe to many, manifesting as a seemingly insurmountable wall between us and our tasks. However, understanding this behaviour is the first step toward overcoming it. This chapter aims to dissect the complexities of procrastination, helping you identify its roots and recognise its various forms in your life. Only then will we move on to resolving these issues and moving forward to a life free from procrastination.

What is Procrastination?

Mark, a software developer, had always labelled himself as lazy due to his chronic procrastination. Deadlines were perpetually daunting, and no matter how straightforward the project, he found himself scrambling at the last minute, leading to sleepless nights and rushed work. This self-assigned laziness confused him because outside of work, he was energetic and ambitious, always tinkering with new programming languages or engaging in complex, time-consuming hobbies.

Research by Klingsieck (2013) emphasises that procrastination is not merely a delay but a dysfunctional behaviour characterised by irrational delays, often accompanied by negative consequences. This is distinct from strategic delay, which is a more functional and intentional postponement of tasks. Procrastinators often experience discomfort and stress due to their delayed actions, as procrastination typically serves as a coping mechanism for emotional regulation, such as avoiding anxiety or fear of failure.

It wasn't until a workshop on workplace efficiency that Mark had his revelation. The facilitator introduced the concept of procrastination as a psychological issue tied to emotion management rather than mere laziness. This concept struck a chord with Mark. He realised that his procrastination was not due to a lack of motivation but rather a fear of failure. Each project's beginning signalled a risk of not meeting his own high standards, triggering anxiety that he subconsciously avoided by delaying his work.

The workshop helped Mark understand that his "laziness" was actually a protective mechanism against this anxiety. Armed with this new understanding, he began to approach his procrastination differently. Instead of berating himself for lack of effort, he focused on managing his anxiety through better planning and setting realistic expectations for his work.

Recognising the true root of his procrastination transformed how Mark worked. He started projects earlier, broke them down into manageable parts, and celebrated small successes along the way. This not only improved his work performance but also significantly reduced his stress levels, making his job more enjoyable and fulfilling.

Procrastination is not just delaying tasks; it is a complex psychological behaviour that involves prioritising less urgent and more enjoyable tasks over more critical ones. It's not a sign of laziness but often a strategy for dealing with the anxiety associated with starting or completing tasks. By understanding that procrastination is a coping mechanism rather than a personal flaw, we can begin to approach it with more empathy and less judgement.

Psychological Roots of Procrastination

Janie had always been known as the 'last-minute planner' among her friends and colleagues. At work, she was the person who turned in projects just before deadlines, and her work, while good, often lacked the polish of thorough review. This pattern had shadowed her from her college days, when late nights before exams were her routine.

Initially, Janie didn't see this as a problem; she felt it was just how she operated best. However, when she received a promotion that required higher levels of planning and team coordination, her habitual procrastination started to become a significant impediment. Tasks began piling up, her stress levels soared, and the quality of her work suffered.

During a particularly overwhelming project, Janie missed a critical deadline that affected her entire team. The feedback from her supervisor was disheartening but eye-opening. She realised that her procrastination was not a quirk of her personality but a serious issue that needed addressing. Seeking to understand why she procrastinated, Janie turned to a psychologist who helped her explore the psychological roots of her behaviour.

Through sessions with her psychologist, Janie discovered that her procrastination stemmed from deep-seated fears of failure and judgement. Subconsciously, she delayed her tasks to avoid confronting these fears. Understanding this was a revelation for Janie. It wasn't just about managing time; it was about managing her anxiety and self-doubt.

Equipped with this new understanding, Janie began applying strategies to tackle her procrastination. She learned techniques for emotional regulation, such as mindfulness and cognitive restructuring to challenge her irrational beliefs about failure and perfection. Gradually, she started facing tasks earlier, setting personal deadlines, and breaking larger projects into manageable parts.

Janie's journey of overcoming procrastination began with understanding its psychological underpinnings. As she continued to apply her new skills, not only did her work improve, but she also experienced less stress and more satisfaction with her career. This change did not happen overnight, but each step forward proved to her that understanding and addressing the root causes of procrastination could transform both her professional life and her personal well-being.

The psychological roots of procrastination are deeply entwined with our emotional responses to tasks and expectations. These emotional responses are often complex and can significantly influence our behaviour in both overt and subtle ways. Here, we look more closely at two key emotional factors that contribute to procrastination: fear of failure and fear of success.

Fear of Failure

Fear of failure is one of the most common causes of procrastination. It involves an underlying worry or anxiety that one's efforts will not yield successful results or that these results will not meet personal or external standards. This fear often stems from:

- Perfectionism: Individuals who strive for perfection may fear undertaking tasks they cannot complete flawlessly. They might believe that anything less than perfect is a failure, which can paralyse their ability to start or progress through tasks.

- Past Experiences: Negative feedback or previous failures can condition someone to avoid similar situations to escape the associated feelings of disappointment or embarrassment.

- Low Self-Esteem: People with low self-esteem might doubt their skills or abilities, leading them to avoid tasks where they anticipate failure, which might reinforce their negative self-image.

When people are afraid they will fail, they might subconsciously choose to avoid starting a task, as not beginning protects them from the possibility of failure. By not attempting, they cannot fail, thus, in a twisted sense, they feel they are maintaining their self-esteem and avoiding the pain of potential failure.

Fear of Success

Ironically, fear of success is another emotional root of procrastination. While it might seem counterintuitive to fear positive outcomes, this fear is associated with the uncertainties and changes that success might bring, such as:

- Increased Expectations: Success can lead to heightened expectations for future performance. For some, the prospect of having to continually meet these increased expectations can be daunting.

- Change in Social Dynamics: Achieving success might alter an individual's role or status within a group, which can lead to anxiety about changing relationships or increased scrutiny from others.

- Self-Identity Concerns: Some individuals might fear that success will change how they are perceived or how they perceive themselves. They might be uncomfortable with the identity of being "successful" due to internal conflicts or perceived external pressures.

People who procrastinate because they fear success often do so because they are concerned about the aftermath of achieving their goals. They might worry about being unable to handle future responsibilities or about being alienated from their current peer group.

Addressing These Fears

Understanding these fears is crucial because it allows individuals to address the root cause of their procrastination rather than just the symptoms. Effective strategies might include:

- Cognitive Behavioral Therapy (CBT): This can help reframe the negative thought patterns that contribute to fears of failure and success.

- Setting Realistic Goals: By setting achievable goals, individuals can build confidence and reduce the pressure associated with outcomes.

- Seeking Feedback: Constructive feedback can help individuals understand and learn from failures and successes in a healthy way.

By exploring and addressing these psychological roots, individuals can better manage their procrastination and move towards a more productive and fulfilling life.

Coping Styles: Adaptive vs. Avoidant Copers

In addition to addressing the psychological roots of procrastination, it's important to recognise how individuals respond emotionally and behaviorally. Research has shown that different coping styles can either help or hinder progress, with most people falling into one of two categories: adaptive or avoidant coping styles. Understanding your coping style can offer insight into why you procrastinate and how to combat it.

Adaptive Copers

Adaptive copers tend to face procrastination head-on by using proactive techniques that help them stay organised and focused. These individuals are more likely to use task management strategies like time-blocking, breaking down tasks into smaller steps, and setting realistic deadlines.

According to Sirois and Pychyl (2013), adaptive copers often succeed in managing procrastination because they focus on long-term goals and maintain a balanced perspective on their tasks. By breaking tasks into smaller, manageable pieces and using structured schedules, adaptive copers reduce the feeling of overwhelm that often leads to procrastination. For example, someone who practises time-blocking might allocate specific hours each day to work on a project, preventing last-minute rushes and reducing stress.

Avoidant Copers

On the other hand, avoidant copers tend to procrastinate as a way to avoid uncomfortable emotions, such as fear, anxiety, or the possibility of failure. Ferrari et al. (1995) identified that avoidant coping often involves engaging in distractions or delaying tactics to escape the negative feelings associated with starting or completing a task. This emotional avoidance can result in chronic procrastination, especially when tasks are linked to high-stakes outcomes.

Avoidant copers often find themselves stuck in a cycle of avoidance, which increases stress as deadlines approach. The fear of failure or judgment becomes so overwhelming that they delay tasks, hoping that the problem will go away. Unfortunately, this only amplifies anxiety, leading to rushed, last-minute efforts that rarely reflect the individual's true capabilities.

Moving Toward Adaptive Coping

For individuals who recognise avoidant coping in their behaviour, there are practical strategies to transition toward adaptive coping styles. Cognitive Behavioural Therapy (CBT), for example, can help reframe negative thought patterns, making tasks feel less threatening. Additionally, mindfulness practices, as explored by Shapiro et al. (2008), help individuals stay grounded in the present, reducing anxiety about future outcomes.

By adopting adaptive strategies like setting achievable goals, focusing on small wins, and creating structure in their daily routines, avoidant copers can gradually reduce procrastination and regain control over their work and personal lives.

Behavioural Aspects of Procrastination

The behavioural aspects of procrastination focus on how this tendency can evolve into a habitual response, driven by certain patterns and triggers in our environment or our routines. Here's a deeper look into how this process unfolds and how it can be addressed.

Habit Formation

Procrastination can become ingrained as a habit through repeated cycles of avoidance. Here's how this cycle typically develops:

1. Initial Avoidance: It starts with a decision to avoid a specific task due to associated discomfort, whether it's due to fear of failure, lack of interest, or perceived difficulty.

2. Temporary Relief: Avoiding the task provides immediate, short-term relief from the discomfort, which serves as a reward and reinforces the avoidance behaviour.

3. Repetition: As this cycle repeats, the brain begins to associate the task with negative feelings and avoidance with relief, strengthening the habit. The more frequently this pattern is repeated, the more entrenched the habit becomes.

4. Automatic Response: Eventually, the response to procrastinate becomes automatic. When faced with a similar task or situation, the individual instinctively opts to procrastinate without much conscious thought, driven by the established habit loop.

Breaking this cycle requires conscious effort and strategies aimed at both understanding and altering these habitual responses.

Triggers and Cues

Identifying the specific triggers that lead to procrastination is crucial for modifying this behaviour. Common triggers include:

- Overwhelming Tasks: Tasks that seem large, complex, or insurmountable can trigger procrastination. The mere thought of tackling such tasks can feel daunting, prompting a delay.

- Uncomfortable Work Environment: An environment that is not conducive to focus and productivity, whether it's noisy, cluttered, or associated with stress, can lead people to procrastinate to avoid discomfort.

- Lack of Clear Goals or Deadlines: Without specific deadlines or clear goals, the urgency to complete tasks is reduced, making it easier to procrastinate.

- Negative Emotional States: Feelings of boredom, anxiety, or low energy can act as triggers. When people feel down or anxious, they may avoid tasks that seem to require a high level of mental or physical energy.

- Perfectionism: The pressure to deliver perfect results can be paralysing, causing delays in starting or completing tasks due to fear of imperfect outcomes.

Addressing Behavioural Aspects

To combat these behavioural aspects of procrastination, consider implementing the following strategies:

- Task Breakdown: Break large, overwhelming tasks into smaller, manageable parts to reduce the psychological barrier to starting.

- Environment Optimisation: Create a workspace that minimises distractions and discomfort, tailored to encourage focus and productivity.

- Set Clear Goals and Deadlines: Clearly defined goals and deadlines can increase accountability and create a sense of urgency, reducing the temptation to procrastinate.

- Mood Management: Techniques such as exercise, meditation, or engaging in a hobby can help improve emotional states and reduce the likelihood of procrastination triggered by negative feelings.

- Challenge Perfectionism: Encourage realistic standards rather than perfection. Setting achievable benchmarks can decrease the anxiety related to performance and reduce procrastination.

Understanding and addressing these behavioural aspects through targeted strategies can significantly reduce the habit of procrastination, leading to improved productivity and satisfaction.

The Impact of Procrastination

Marcus, a talented graphic designer known for his creativity, faced a harsh reality check due to his chronic procrastination. With a freelance career that allowed him flexibility and control over his schedule, Marcus often pushed deadlines to the very edge, believing that pressure fueled his creativity. However, this habit took a serious toll when he was given the opportunity to work on a major campaign for a high-profile client—a chance to advance his career significantly.

As the project began, Marcus felt confident. The deadline seemed reasonable, and his initial ideas were met with enthusiasm. But as days turned into weeks, Marcus found himself distracted by less pressing, more comfortable tasks. He told himself he had plenty of time, dismissing the creeping anxiety as typical pre-deadline nerves.

When the final week before the deadline arrived, Marcus was forced to confront the reality that he had grossly underestimated the time required to complete the project. Long nights and chaotic days ensued as he scrambled to consolidate weeks of work into a few frantic sessions. The result was a product that fell far short of his usual standards.

The presentation was a disaster. The client was visibly disappointed, noting the lack of polish and depth in the work that had seemed so promising in the initial pitches. The feedback was a professional blow for Marcus, resulting in him not only losing that account but also damaging his reputation in a tightly-knit industry.

This painful experience forced Marcus to reflect deeply on how his procrastination had not only jeopardised his career but also his self-esteem and mental health. Stress, anxiety, and a plummeting self-image followed as he grappled with the fallout. Realising the need for change, Marcus sought help from a productivity coach, learned to set realistic micro-goals, and gradually rebuilt his approach to work.

Marcus's story exemplifies the destructive potential of unchecked procrastination. It serves as a stark reminder of the concrete losses—professional opportunities, personal reputation, and mental well-being—that can result from the habit. His journey towards recovery and reformation highlights the importance of confronting procrastination head-on, transforming damaging habits into a disciplined, proactive approach to both work and life.

The impact of procrastination extends beyond mere delays in completing tasks; it seeps into various aspects of life, causing significant repercussions that can undermine personal growth, health, and well-being. Let's look more closely at how procrastination can profoundly affect personal goals, mental health, and physical health.

On Personal Goals

Procrastination poses a serious threat to the achievement of personal goals. When tasks are continually postponed:

- Missed Opportunities: Opportunities for advancement, whether in a career, education, or personal projects, may be lost due to missed deadlines or poor preparation. For instance, a student who procrastinates on studying might perform poorly on exams, affecting their academic progress, or a professional might miss a project deadline, resulting in lost job opportunities or promotions.

- Cycle of Regret: Each instance of procrastination can lead to regret, which compounds over time. This regret can manifest as self-blame and a persistent feeling of disappointment, particularly when reflecting on what could have been achieved if time had been managed better.

- Stagnation: Chronic procrastination can lead to a lack of personal development and stagnation. When individuals fail to act toward their goals, they miss out on developing skills and experiences that are crucial for personal growth and satisfaction.

On Mental Health

The psychological effects of procrastination are significant and multifaceted:

- Increased Stress and Anxiety: As deadlines approach or tasks accumulate, the stress and anxiety of needing to meet these compressed timelines can be overwhelming. This stress is not just momentary; it can build into chronic anxiety as the habit of procrastination persists.

- Lowered Self-Esteem: Regular procrastination can lead to feelings of inadequacy and failure, which erode self-esteem. When individuals repeatedly fail to meet their own expectations or those of others, they may begin to view themselves as incapable or unworthy, perpetuating a negative self-image.

- Mental Exhaustion: The constant cycle of urgency, stress, and regret that accompanies procrastination can lead to mental exhaustion. This can impair cognitive functions like decision-making and problem-solving, further reducing productivity and effectiveness.

On Physical Health

The physiological impacts of procrastination often mirror the intensity of its psychological effects:

- Headaches and Muscle Tension: Stress and anxiety stemming from procrastination can lead to physical symptoms such as headaches and muscle tension, especially in the neck, shoulders, and back. These symptoms are not only painful but can also distract from focus and productivity.

- Sleep Disturbances: The stress associated with unfinished tasks can disrupt sleep patterns, leading to difficulties in falling asleep, sleep disturbances, or insomnia. Poor sleep can exacerbate the cycle of stress and procrastination, creating a feedback loop that is hard to break.

- Weakened Immune System: Chronic stress can weaken the immune system, making the body more susceptible to infections. Habitual procrastinators may find themselves getting sick more often, further impacting their ability to complete tasks and achieve goals.

The far-reaching consequences of procrastination illustrate why it is crucial to address this behaviour head-on. Understanding these impacts can motivate individuals to seek effective strategies and interventions to break the cycle of procrastination, thus improving their productivity, mental and physical health, and overall quality of life.

Procrastination in Everyday Life

Emily was an ambitious marketing coordinator in a bustling agency, known for her creative ideas and strong work ethic. However, her hidden struggle with procrastination often put her at odds with her professional aspirations. Despite her talents, Emily had a habit of delaying tasks, especially those that required her to present her work to others, due to her fear of criticism.

The consequences of her procrastination came to a head during a major campaign pitch. Emily had brilliant ideas for the campaign, but she delayed organising her thoughts and preparing the presentation, convincing herself she worked better under pressure. As the pitch day approached, she found herself overwhelmed, scrambling to put everything together at the last minute.

On the day of the presentation, Emily was not only physically exhausted from working through the night but also mentally scattered. Her presentation was underdeveloped, and her delivery lacked the usual confidence that characterised her work. The pitch did not go well. The client was unimpressed, leading to the loss of a potentially lucrative account for her firm.

This incident was a wake-up call for Emily. The fallout from the failed pitch was severe—her team's morale dipped, and her manager expressed disappointment in what had happened. Emily realised that her procrastination was not a benign quirk but a serious impediment that was costing her professionally and affecting her team.

Determined to change, Emily sought help. She began working with a productivity coach to understand the root of her procrastination and developed strategies to manage her workload effectively. She learned to break down tasks into manageable steps, set realistic deadlines, and seek feedback early in the process to avoid last-minute panics.

Months later, Emily had another opportunity to lead a campaign pitch. This time, she was ready. She started her preparations early, sought input from her colleagues along the way, and fine-tuned her presentation until it was polished. The pitch was a success, not only securing the account but also restoring her reputation within her team.

Emily's story is a testament to how recognising and addressing procrastination can transform challenges into victories. Her journey from a problematic pitch to a successful one illustrates the importance of confronting procrastination head-on and taking proactive steps to overcome it.

Procrastination is a common challenge that affects many aspects of daily life, from academic and workplace settings to personal commitments. By examining how procrastination manifests in these areas, we can better understand its impacts and develop strategies to overcome it.

Academic Procrastination

In academic environments, procrastination is particularly prevalent. Many students delay starting assignments until the last minute, a behaviour that can significantly affect their grades and overall learning experience. This type of procrastination often stems from a fear of failure or a lack of confidence in one's abilities. Students may also procrastinate due to feeling overwhelmed by the task's perceived difficulty or a general disinterest in the subject matter.

To combat academic procrastination, students can break assignments into smaller, manageable parts and set mini-deadlines for each segment. Establishing a regular study schedule and creating a conducive study environment are also key strategies. Recognising and addressing the underlying fears or lack of interest that lead to procrastination can additionally help students stay engaged and timely with their coursework.

Workplace Procrastination

In the workplace, procrastination can have far-reaching effects on productivity and team dynamics. Delaying tasks can lead to missed deadlines, decreased work quality, and increased stress for both the individual and their team members. Workplace procrastination often occurs when tasks are ambiguous or when an employee feels disconnected from the outcomes of their work.

Managers can help reduce workplace procrastination by clearly defining task responsibilities, providing regular feedback, and ensuring employees understand the impact of their work on the broader organisational goals. Individuals can also mitigate procrastination by improving their time management skills, setting clear daily priorities, and seeking support when needed.

Personal Procrastination

On a personal level, procrastination can strain relationships and hinder personal growth. Delaying important life decisions, such as starting an exercise routine or saving for retirement, can have long-term consequences. Similarly, procrastinating on day-to-day responsibilities, like paying bills or maintaining a home, can lead to unnecessary stress and complications.

To address personal procrastination, it is helpful to understand the emotional or logistical barriers that are causing the delay. Implementing a reward system for completing personal tasks, scheduling specific times for these activities, and enlisting support from friends or family can motivate individuals to take action more promptly.

Understanding the specific ways in which procrastination impacts different areas of life can provide valuable insights into why individuals delay tasks and how they can develop more effective coping strategies. Whether it's in academic settings, the workplace, or personal life, tackling procrastination involves a combination of strategic planning, understanding the psychological underpinnings, and actively making changes to one's approach to tasks and responsibilities. By addressing procrastination head-on in these everyday scenarios, individuals can improve their efficiency, achieve their goals, and enhance their overall quality of life.

Complex Interplay

Understanding procrastination is not merely about identifying a bad habit; it's about uncovering a complex interplay of psychological, behavioural, and situational factors that influence how and why we delay tasks. This initial exploration into the roots of procrastination provides you with the critical insights necessary to begin the transformative process of change.

As we delve deeper into this book, the knowledge you've acquired here will act as a solid foundation for the practical strategies discussed in subsequent chapters. Each section is designed to build upon the last, forming a comprehensive guide that will equip you with the tools to not just fight procrastination but also understand and manage it effectively.

The goal of this journey is not to eradicate procrastination entirely—a feat that is both unrealistic and unnecessary. Instead, our aim is to manage it in a way that aligns with your personal and professional aspirations. By doing so, you regain control over your actions and, by extension, your life. This control is crucial for achieving your goals and fulfilling your potential.

Remember, every piece of knowledge you gain and every strategy you implement is a step toward greater productivity and a more engaged life. The power to change your habits and overcome procrastination lies in your hands. As you move forward, keep in mind that small, consistent efforts lead to significant transformations. Let this understanding empower you to take action, make informed decisions, and progressively reclaim the hours lost to procrastination.

By managing procrastination effectively, you open up new opportunities for success and satisfaction in all areas of your life. This is not just about completing tasks; it's about enhancing your quality of life and achieving a sense of accomplishment and well-being. So, embrace this journey with an open mind and a commitment to apply what you learn. The tools and strategies provided here are designed to guide you, but it is your actions that will ultimately transform these ideas into tangible results.

Reflective Questions:

- What tasks or responsibilities do you tend to delay the most, and why?

- When you procrastinate, what emotions do you typically feel (e.g., anxiety, fear, or boredom)?

Actionable Takeaways:

- Identify one major task you've been avoiding. Break it down into smaller, more manageable steps, and start working on the first step today.

Challenge:

Spend the next three days tracking the tasks you procrastinate on. Use a journal or app to note when you delay tasks, how long you procrastinate, and what activities you engage in instead. Reflect on the emotional or psychological triggers that led to the procrastination.

Psychological Barriers and How to Overcome Them

Lisa, a talented but reserved software developer, faced a daunting psychological barrier: her intense anxiety around public speaking. Early in her career, just the thought of presenting in front of colleagues triggered a deep-seated fear. This anxiety wasn't merely a case of nerves; it was a profound dread that paralysed her, making the simplest preparations seem insurmountable.

Her first team presentation was a pivotal moment. Despite knowing it was crucial for her career, Lisa's fear led her to procrastinate on preparing. She hoped that delaying would somehow make the necessity of the task disappear. Instead, this lack of preparation ensured she was unpracticed and ill-prepared, leading to a self-fulfilling prophecy. During the presentation, she stumbled over her words and struggled to communicate her ideas clearly. Her slides, hastily thrown together, did not convey the innovative work she had done. The experience was mortifying and it deepened her dread, trapping her in a cycle where anxiety fuelled procrastination, which in turn, only heightened her anxiety.

Procrastination often stems from cognitive patterns that emphasise the past rather than future-oriented goals. Specter and Ferrari (2000) revealed that chronic procrastinators are more focused on their past accomplishments or failures, which negatively impacts their ability to plan for future tasks. These tendencies often result in avoidant behaviour and missed deadlines. Lisa, too, was trapped in this cycle, focusing more on the fear of replicating past failures than preparing for future success.

Determined to break this cycle, Lisa recognised that she needed to confront her fear directly but gradually. She started by seeking roles that required minimal public speaking but still pushed her out of her comfort zone. She volunteered to lead small, informal meetings within her department. These settings, while still challenging, were less intimidating due to the familiar faces and supportive atmosphere. This initial step was critical—it was about proving to herself that she could handle the anxiety in controlled doses.

As her comfort with these smaller groups grew, so did her confidence. Lisa then began to extend her reach, offering to present parts of projects during inter-departmental meetings. Each successful engagement, no matter how small, was a victory. It was during these presentations that she started refining her skills in organising her thoughts and engaging her audience, which gradually made the idea of larger presentations less formidable.

Fuelled by these incremental successes, Lisa took a significant step forward: she enrolled in a public speaking workshop. The structured environment of the workshop provided her with concrete strategies to structure her speeches and manage her nervousness. She learned techniques such as deep breathing, focusing on the message rather than the audience's reaction, and how to effectively organise her content to hold the audience's interest.

Her transformation reached its peak when her team was selected to present at a major industry conference. This was the moment Lisa had been building towards, turning her once paralysing fear into a potential career highlight. She prepared meticulously, practised her speech repeatedly, and visualised her success. On the day of the conference, she stood before over two hundred industry professionals and delivered a compelling, confident presentation on her team's innovative project. The positive feedback was overwhelming, not just for the quality of her work but for her clear, confident delivery.

Lisa's journey from a fearful speaker to a confident presenter is a testament to the power of gradual exposure and persistence in overcoming psychological barriers. By starting in less intimidating environments and methodically building up to bigger stages, Lisa transformed her approach to public speaking. What was once a weakness had become a celebrated strength, proving that with the right strategies and a commitment to growth, even the most daunting fears can be conquered.

Overcoming procrastination isn't just about improving time management skills; it's fundamentally about confronting and transforming the psychological barriers that inhibit action. This chapter delves into common psychological hurdles—fear and anxiety, self-image issues, and difficulties with emotional regulation—and provides strategies to overcome them effectively.

Fear and Anxiety

Fear and anxiety are not just fleeting emotions; they are powerful forces that can dictate our actions—or, in the case of procrastination, our inactions. When fear takes root, it can paralyse decision-making and delay the tasks we find most daunting. Understanding and addressing these fears is crucial for moving forward and reclaiming control over your productivity.

Reframing Fear

The fear of failure is pervasive and can be a significant roadblock. It often stems from the misconception that failure is inherently bad, a marker of personal inadequacy. However, reframing how you view failure can dramatically alter your approach to work and challenges. Consider failure not as a setback but as a vital component of growth. Each failure is a lesson in disguise, offering invaluable insights into what does not work and paving the way for improved strategies.

A profound example of this in practice is found in the story of Thomas Edison and his quest to develop the incandescent light bulb. As one of the most prolific inventors in history, he didn't see failure as most do. His journey to invent the incandescent light bulb was filled with thousands of unsuccessful attempts. Throughout these trials, he encountered numerous setbacks, each one a potential reason to give up. However, Edison chose to view each "failure" not as a fruitless endeavour, but as a vital step toward his goal. He famously said, "I have not failed. I've just found 10,000 ways that won't work."

Edison's perspective on failure is a classic example of how reframing the concept of failure can lead to remarkable achievements. Rather than perceiving each unsuccessful attempt as a defeat, he saw each as an opportunity to learn something new. This mindset allowed him to persist where others might have given up, ultimately leading to the successful creation of the light bulb, which has had a profound and lasting impact on the world.

Edison's approach illustrates the power of persistence and positive framing. His ability to persistently view each setback as a lesson rather than a failure paved the way for the invention of the light bulb and set a precedent for how modern inventors and entrepreneurs approach innovation. His story encourages us to view our own setbacks and challenges as integral to the learning process, teaching us resilience and problem-solving skills that are crucial in any successful endeavour.

Similarly, the fear of success, though less discussed, is equally debilitating for some. This fear usually arises from underlying beliefs that success will lead to negative outcomes like increased pressure, jealousy from peers, or a loss of current lifestyle. To combat this, it's essential to identify these beliefs and challenge them. Ask yourself: Are these outcomes inevitable, or are they perceptions that can be managed? More often than not, the benefits of success and overcoming challenges outweigh the perceived drawbacks.

Exposure Therapy

As with Lisa's journey, a practical approach to overcoming fear is gradual exposure. Start by identifying the tasks that ignite your anxiety. Break these tasks down into smaller, less intimidating components and tackle them one at a time. For instance, if public speaking makes you anxious, start by speaking in front of a mirror, then to a small group of friends, and gradually increase the audience size. This method helps build confidence progressively and diminishes the overall anxiety associated with the task.

Mindfulness and Relaxation Techniques

Implementing mindfulness and relaxation techniques can provide immediate relief from anxiety symptoms and help manage stress in the long run. Techniques such as deep breathing, meditation, and progressive muscle relaxation can be incorporated into your daily routine to help calm your mind and reduce the physical symptoms of anxiety. These practices encourage a state of awareness and present-mindedness, allowing you to focus on the task at hand rather than being consumed by worry about the future or past failures.

By addressing fear and anxiety with these practical strategies, you can begin to dismantle the psychological barriers that lead to procrastination. Each step you take to confront your fears boosts your confidence and enhances your ability to engage with your tasks more effectively and with less apprehension.

Self-Image and Self-Compassion

Jordan was a skilled graphic designer who secretly struggled with a harsh self-image. Despite his obvious talent and positive feedback from colleagues, he habitually downplayed his successes and fixated on any small errors. This negative self-perception was rooted in early educational experiences where he was often compared unfavourably to his peers, leading him to internalise a belief that he was not good enough.

This crippling self-doubt led Jordan to procrastinate on projects, especially those that required him to showcase his work publicly or assume leadership roles. Fearful of confirming his perceived inadequacies, he would delay beginning projects until the last possible moment, often compromising on quality due to time constraints.

The turning point came when Jordan's supervisor noticed his struggles and suggested he might benefit from professional help. Jordan started therapy, where he learned that his procrastination was a protective mechanism against perceived failure and judgement. Through cognitive-behavioural therapy (CBT), he began to challenge his long-held negative beliefs about his abilities, replacing them with more realistic and positive assessments.

Additionally, Jordan joined a peer support group for professionals dealing with similar issues. Sharing his experiences and hearing others' stories helped him realise he was not alone in his feelings of inadequacy. The group provided a safe space to receive constructive feedback, which gradually helped rebuild his confidence.

As therapy and peer support helped Jordan foster greater self-compassion, he noticed a significant shift in his professional behaviour. He started volunteering for challenging projects, engaging more with his team, and taking on leadership roles he would have previously shunned. Each successful project under these new conditions reinforced his positive self-image and reduced his need to procrastinate as a defence mechanism.

Jordan's story exemplifies how addressing deep-seated issues with self-image through therapy and community support can dramatically transform one's professional life. By learning to challenge negative narratives and practice self-compassion,

Jordan not only improved his work performance but also his overall well-being and satisfaction with his career.

How we view ourselves deeply influences our approach to tasks and challenges. Negative self-perceptions can be a powerful catalyst for procrastination, as they often convince us that we are not capable or deserving of success. By transforming how we see ourselves and how we treat ourselves in moments of struggle, we can overcome these mental barriers and adopt a more productive and fulfilling approach to work and life.

Building a Positive Self-Image

The foundation of a strong self-image lies in recognising and appreciating your strengths and achievements. One practical method to enhance your self-image is by maintaining a "success journal." Regularly write down your accomplishments, no matter how small they may seem. This could be anything from completing a task you've been postponing to receiving positive feedback at work. Over time, reviewing this journal can significantly boost your confidence and reinforce a positive perception of your abilities.

Moreover, actively seek out and embrace new challenges as opportunities to learn and expand your skills. Each challenge you overcome not only adds to your success journal but also solidifies your belief in your capability to handle future obstacles.

Practising Self-Compassion

Self-compassion is about treating yourself with the same kindness and understanding that you would offer a good friend. Start by becoming more mindful of your self-talk. Are you overly critical of yourself? Do you dwell on your shortcomings? Begin to consciously replace negative or self-critical thoughts with more supportive and compassionate messages. For example, instead of telling yourself, "I always mess things up," you might say, "I can learn from my mistakes and improve."

Remember, self-compassion is not about making excuses for your shortcomings but about acknowledging them without harsh judgement. This shift in mindset can reduce the fear of failure, which often leads to procrastination.

Setting Realistic Expectations

Another aspect of fostering a healthier self-image is setting realistic expectations. Unrealistic standards can set you up for failure, disappointment, and the belief that you are less capable than you actually are. Instead, set achievable goals that challenge you without leading to overwhelming pressure. Recognise that imperfection is a natural part of the human experience and that making mistakes is a critical part of learning and growing.

Adjusting your expectations doesn't mean lowering your standards but rather setting goals that are both challenging and achievable, allowing for personal growth and learning along the way. This approach not only increases your chances of success but also makes the journey towards your goals more enjoyable and less fraught with anxiety.

By focusing on building a positive self-image, practising self-compassion, and setting realistic expectations, you can create a more supportive mental environment. This environment not only fosters personal and professional growth but also minimises the procrastination that stems from fear and self-doubt. Remember, the journey to overcoming procrastination and building a productive life is as much about how you treat yourself as it is about managing your time or tasks.

Emotional Regulation

Effective emotional management is crucial in overcoming the habit of procrastination. Our emotional responses can either propel us towards action or pull us into cycles of delay and avoidance. By understanding and regulating these responses, we can create a more stable foundation for productivity.

Maya, an experienced project manager, found herself frequently overwhelmed by the demands of her job. The pressure to meet deadlines, manage team dynamics, and deliver exceptional results often led to high stress and anxiety. Maya noticed that her emotional state was directly impacting her productivity: the more stressed she felt, the more she procrastinated, fearing she wouldn't meet her own high standards.

Realising that her emotional responses were at the core of her procrastination habits, Maya began exploring mindfulness techniques. She started with guided meditations, initially focusing on just breathing and being present in the moment. This simple practice helped her become more aware of her emotional triggers and the physical sensations associated with stress.

As Maya became more adept at recognising when her emotions were beginning to spiral, she incorporated mindfulness into her daily routine. Before starting work, she would take ten minutes to meditate, setting a calm and focused tone for the day. She also used mindfulness breaks during the day whenever she felt overwhelmed or noticed the urge to procrastinate. These breaks involved a few minutes of deep breathing or a short walk, allowing her to clear her mind and reset her emotional state.

These mindfulness practices had a transformative effect on Maya. By managing her emotions more effectively, she reduced the frequency and intensity of her procrastination. She found herself starting tasks sooner, with a clearer mind and a more balanced approach to her work. Her team noticed the change too; Maya's calm demeanour and enhanced focus fostered a more positive and productive work environment.

Moreover, the benefits of mindfulness extended beyond her professional life. Maya experienced improvements in her sleep quality and overall well-being, feeling less anxious and more in control of her life. Her journey through emotional regulation via mindfulness not only curbed her procrastination but also significantly enhanced her personal and professional satisfaction.

Maya's story highlights how integrating mindfulness into daily life can be a powerful tool for regulating emotions, combating procrastination, and improving overall well-being.

Identifying Emotional Triggers

The first step towards emotional regulation is to identify what triggers your procrastination. Keeping a detailed diary where you log each instance of procrastination can be incredibly insightful. Note what you were supposed to do, what you did instead, and how you felt before and after the procrastination occurred. Over time, patterns will emerge. You may find that certain types of tasks, times of day, or emotional states consistently lead to procrastination. Understanding these patterns is the first step in managing them effectively.

Cognitive Behavioral Techniques

Cognitive Behavioral Therapy (CBT) techniques are particularly effective in addressing the irrational thoughts and beliefs that fuel emotional distress. If you find yourself procrastinating due to fears of inadequacy, or beliefs that your work will not be good enough, CBT techniques can help you challenge these thoughts and replace them with more realistic and balanced ones. For example, if you believe, "If I can't do this perfectly, then it's a complete failure," you could reframe this to "Any progress on this task is a step forward, and mistakes are opportunities for learning."

Implementing CBT involves recognising negative thought patterns, disputing their validity, and then consciously forming and strengthening alternative, more positive thoughts. This process not only alleviates anxiety and guilt associated with procrastination but also empowers you to approach tasks with a healthier mindset.

Developing Resilience

Building resilience is about enhancing your ability to cope with the ups and downs of life without falling into prolonged procrastination. This can be achieved by setting small, achievable goals that create frequent opportunities for success. Each small success builds your confidence and establishes a positive feedback loop, making you less likely to procrastinate and more likely to feel capable of tackling challenging tasks.

Additionally, resilience can be bolstered by maintaining a supportive network and engaging in regular self-reflection. Reflecting on how you've overcome past obstacles or how you've managed to progress despite challenges can reinforce a sense of competence and perseverance.

By focusing on these strategies—identifying emotional triggers, applying cognitive behavioural techniques, and developing resilience—you equip yourself with the tools to manage your emotional landscape more effectively. This helps overcome procrastination and enhances your overall well-being, leading to a more productive and fulfilling personal and professional life. Embrace these strategies as part of a continuous growth journey, not as quick fixes but as lifelong adjustments to how you interact with your emotions and tasks.

Develop Understanding

Overcoming the psychological barriers to action is not about suppressing your true feelings or changing who you are. Instead, it's about developing a deeper understanding of yourself, building resilience, and learning to navigate your emotions more effectively. By addressing these barriers, you open up a pathway to more productive behaviours and a more fulfilling life.

Reflective Questions:

- Are fear or anxiety playing a role in your procrastination? What specific fears are holding you back?

- How often do you delay tasks because of perfectionism or fear of failure?

Actionable Takeaways:

- Identify one small action you can take today to confront a task that scares you. Don't worry about perfect results, just focus on taking action.

Challenge:

Identify one task you've been avoiding because of fear or anxiety. Over the next week, break it down into two or three small, manageable steps. Complete just the first step. Afterward, reflect on how you feel and whether the task was as daunting as you initially thought.

Practical Strategies to Beat Procrastination

Procrastination isn't just a mental barrier; it often stems from not knowing where or how to start. This chapter introduces practical strategies designed to transform your approach to tasks and projects, making them more manageable and less daunting. By setting small goals, organising tasks effectively, and mastering time management, you can create a framework that systematically dismantles the habit of procrastination.

Setting Small and Achievable Goals

When faced with a daunting task, the size and scope can often lead to paralysis, where even starting seems impossible. However, the key to overcoming this inertia lies in breaking the task into smaller, more manageable parts. This approach not only makes the task seem less intimidating but also provides a clear path forward, helping you build momentum as you progress.

Break It Down

The first step in tackling a large task is to deconstruct it into its component parts. For example, if your project is to write a comprehensive report, start by segmenting the process: research, outline, write, and review. By dividing it in this way, you focus only on the next immediate step rather than the entire project. This segmentation simplifies your focus and reduces anxiety, making it easier to start and maintain progress.

Consider using visual aids like flow charts or lists to map out these steps. Seeing them laid out before you can demystify the process and give you a tangible roadmap to follow.

Set Mini-Deadlines

For each segment you've identified, set realistic mini-deadlines. These serve as checkpoints that help you stay on track and prevent last-minute rushes. Mini-deadlines also create a series of manageable goals rather than a single, looming deadline. This approach helps maintain a steady pace of work, and each deadline met serves as a mini victory, propelling you forward.

Effective use of a calendar or digital reminders can ensure you're aware of these deadlines as they approach, helping keep your tasks front and centre in your daily planning.

Celebrate Small Wins

Every time you complete a task segment, take a moment to acknowledge and celebrate this achievement. Whether it's a small reward like a coffee break or a short walk, or simply taking a moment to reflect on the progress made, celebrating these wins is crucial. This positive reinforcement not only boosts your morale but also increases your motivation to tackle the next segment of the task.

This celebration of small victories keeps the journey towards completing a big task light and enjoyable, rather than a long slog to the finish line. It changes the narrative from enduring a marathon to enjoying a series of short, rewarding sprints.

By implementing these strategies—breaking tasks down, setting mini-deadlines, and celebrating small wins—you can transform overwhelming projects into a series of achievable steps. This approach not only reduces procrastination but also enhances your overall productivity and satisfaction with your work. Embrace the philosophy that every large task, no matter how daunting, can be conquered one small step at a time.

When my business partner presented me with the daunting challenge of improving the productivity of a pressure-diecasting machine by 5%, I was initially overwhelmed. The project required not just enhancing the machine's speed but also ensuring the safety of operators and the integrity of the car parts it produced. The stakes were incredibly high—dealing with molten metal under massive pressures and extremely high temperatures, any mistake could potentially cost lives.

Previously, I had only worked on control systems for smaller scientific instruments, so the scale and complexity of this task seemed beyond my capabilities. The thought of taking on such a mammoth project was paralysing. My instinct was to focus on less intimidating tasks, as each time I thought about the project, its enormity clouded my belief in my ability to succeed.

However, everything changed when my business partner, confident in my abilities, prematurely sold the project to our largest customer. Suddenly, procrastination was no longer an option; I had to deliver. Faced with no alternative, I turned to the strategy that eventually reshaped my approach to work: breaking down the project into small, manageable tasks.

I started by segmenting the project into several phases:

1. Understanding the Current System: I spent time with the machine, learning its every function and identifying potential areas for efficiency improvements.

2. Designing the Control System: This phase was broken into further small tasks like drafting initial designs, running simulations, and testing components individually.

3. Integration and Testing: Each part of the new system was integrated step by step, testing for both performance and safety.

By focusing on one small task at a time, the project became less intimidating. Each completed task built my confidence and provided a clear path to the next. This step-by-step approach not only kept the project moving forward but also helped maintain a clear focus without being overwhelmed by the broader scope.

Ultimately, the project not only met the initial goal of a 5% increase in productivity but exceeded it spectacularly, achieving a 20% increase. This success significantly boosted my professional reputation and solidified my belief in the power of breaking down overwhelming goals into smaller, achievable steps.

This experience was transformative, teaching me that no project is too large when you approach it one small step at a time. It's a strategy that I have since applied to numerous other projects, each time turning daunting tasks into a series of manageable and often enjoyable achievements. This approach didn't just help me professionally; it changed how I tackled challenges in all areas of my life, leading to the method I later detailed in my book, "Winning the Game," dedicated to the concept of RAPID goal achievement.

Organising Tasks Effectively

Mastering the art of organisation is a crucial strategy in the fight against procrastination. Effective organisation not only clarifies what needs to be done but also reduces the mental clutter that can inhibit starting. By establishing a clear and structured approach to your tasks, you can minimise hesitation and maximise productivity.

Use Lists and Tools

The first step in organising effectively is to utilise tools that suit your style and needs. To-do lists, digital planners, or comprehensive project management software can all serve as valuable aids in keeping track of tasks and deadlines. These tools help you visualise your workload, making tasks seem less abstract and more concrete. When you can clearly see what needs to be done, those tasks become more approachable, and the process of tackling them becomes more systematic.

For instance, a digital planner can remind you of deadlines, help you set reminders for follow-ups, and even block time for deep focus work. The key is to choose a tool that integrates seamlessly with your daily life, ensuring that it enhances rather than complicates your workflow.

Prioritise Wisely

Not all tasks are created equal, and recognising this is critical in managing your workload effectively. Utilising prioritisation techniques such as the Eisenhower Box can be transformative. This method divides tasks into four categories: urgent and important, important but not urgent, urgent but not important, and neither urgent nor important. Such categorisation helps you focus on what truly impacts your goals, allowing you to manage your time and energy more efficiently.

This approach prevents the common pitfall of spending too much time on tasks that may seem urgent—like responding to every email as it arrives—but do little to advance your overall objectives. Instead, it guides you to invest in tasks that contribute to long-term gains.

Regular Review

An often overlooked aspect of organisation is the regular review of your task list and schedules. Set a routine, whether it be daily, weekly, or monthly, to update and review your plans. This habit ensures that your tasks are always current and aligned with your goals. It also provides an opportunity to celebrate completed tasks, which can be a significant motivational boost.

Regular reviews also help you adjust your plans based on new information or changes in priority, keeping your workflow flexible and responsive. This adaptability is key to maintaining efficiency and effectiveness in your endeavours.

By adopting these strategies—utilising tools to keep track of tasks, prioritising effectively, and regularly reviewing your plans—you create a robust framework for productivity. This organised approach not only makes starting tasks less daunting but also keeps you moving forward with a clear sense of direction. Organising tasks effectively is not just about managing your to-dos; it's about clearing a path towards achieving your biggest goals.

Claire, a seasoned content manager at a bustling digital marketing firm, found herself perpetually swamped. Her desk was a landscape of scattered notes and urgent reminders, each piece of paper a ticking time bomb of deadlines. Her computer was no different, with countless digital files haphazardly saved across various folders. This chaos not only hindered her efficiency but significantly magnified her stress levels, leading her to procrastinate. Tasks seemed too daunting to start, and as deadlines approached, her anxiety skyrocketed.

IMPORTANT

U R G E N T	1—Urgent and important	2—Urgent but not important
	3—Important but not urgent	4—Neither important nor urgent

The turning point came when Claire missed a crucial deadline for a high-profile client campaign, resulting in a tense meeting with her supervisors. Realising her disorganisation was jeopardising her career, Claire decided it was time for a change.

Determined to regain control, Claire began her organisational overhaul by adopting a digital project management tool recommended by a colleague. This tool allowed her to visually map out tasks, assign them priorities, and track progress in real-time. She structured her projects into categories, each with subtasks with clear, manageable deadlines.

Claire didn't stop there; she reorganised her digital files with a clear naming convention and dedicated folders for each project, making them easily accessible. Her physical workspace underwent a similar transformation, with a simple, effective filing system and a decluttered desk.

With these systems in place, Claire's approach to work transformed dramatically. The visual layout of tasks helped her see the big picture without feeling overwhelmed. Knowing exactly where everything was saved, both physically and digitally, cut down her preparation time significantly, allowing her to start tasks promptly. As she ticked off each subtask, her confidence grew, and the urge to procrastinate dwindled.

Her newfound efficiency did not go unnoticed. Claire's ability to manage multiple projects smoothly led to her leading more significant campaigns. Her stress levels decreased markedly, and she found herself enjoying work again, invigorated by her ability to tackle challenges head-on.

Claire's transition from chaos to order illustrates the profound impact that effective organisational tools and strategies can have on managing workload and reducing procrastination. By creating an organised workflow, Claire not only enhanced her professional performance but also reclaimed her enthusiasm and confidence in her abilities.

Time Management Essentials

Effective time management is not merely a skill—it is an essential discipline that serves as the backbone of productivity and a vital countermeasure against procrastination. Mastering time management allows you to control your workflow rather than being controlled by it, helping to eliminate the panic of last-minute rushes and the chronic stress that can come from feeling constantly behind schedule.

Time Blocking

One of the most effective time management techniques is time blocking. This involves dividing your day into blocks of time, each dedicated to accomplishing a specific task or group of tasks. Just as you would schedule a meeting in your calendar, schedule your work tasks. This method helps you focus deeply, as you know you only have a set amount of time to work on the task at hand.

Moreover, time blocking helps you maintain a healthy work-life balance by ensuring that you have time set aside not just for work tasks but also for breaks, meals, exercise, and personal time. This structured approach reduces the temptation to overwork and helps keep burnout at bay, making your productive times more effective.

Set Clear Deadlines

Deadlines are powerful motivators. They create a sense of urgency that can help propel you to action. For every task or project, set a clear deadline—even if one is not explicitly required. Self-imposed deadlines can provide structure and momentum, helping you to complete tasks more efficiently. To make these deadlines work, they should be realistic, giving you enough time to do quality work without undue stress, yet tight enough to prevent the task from dragging on indefinitely.

Avoid Multitasking

While multitasking might seem like an efficient use of time, it often leads to diminished focus, lower quality of work, and ultimately, a higher propensity for procrastination. When you split your attention between multiple tasks, none receives your full focus, and tasks can take longer to complete. Instead, embrace the practice of single-tasking. Focus on one task at a time, giving it your undivided attention until it's complete, or until the time block dedicated to it ends. This approach not only improves the quality of your work but also enhances your satisfaction with the work done, as each task completed is an accomplishment in its own right.

By implementing these time management essentials—time blocking, setting clear deadlines, and avoiding multitasking—you lay the groundwork for a more organised, productive, and fulfilling professional life. These strategies are about making the most of the time you have, turning what often feels like an ever-depleting resource into a well-managed asset.

Alex, a freelance graphic designer, had a passion project that he'd been dreaming about for years: creating a comprehensive online course to teach design basics to beginners. Although he was highly motivated by the idea, the vast scope of the project and his irregular freelance schedule led him to put it off continually. Each year, the project remained on his list of New Year's resolutions, untouched and intimidating.

Frustrated by his lack of progress and determined to make his vision a reality, Alex decided to overhaul his approach to time management. He learned about time blocking—a method that involves dedicating specific blocks of time to individual tasks or types of work. Intrigued by the potential to streamline his workflow, Alex meticulously planned his weeks, assigning fixed times for client work, project development, and personal breaks.

He started by setting aside two hours each morning for his course project. During these blocks, he focused solely on tasks related to the course: one day might be for scripting lessons, another for graphic creation, and another for recording videos. He strictly adhered to this schedule, treating these blocks as unmovable appointments with himself.

Alex also implemented strict boundaries for client work, which had previously spilt over into his personal project time. By communicating clear availability times to his clients, he was able to contain his freelance tasks within designated work hours, leaving his mornings free for his course development.

As weeks turned into months, Alex's project, once a source of guilt and frustration, began to take shape. The structured approach helped him make consistent progress without feeling overwhelmed. Each completed segment of the course reinforced his commitment and boosted his morale.

By the end of the year, Alex had not only completed the course but also successfully launched it. The response was overwhelmingly positive, with hundreds of sign-ups and glowing reviews praising the clarity and accessibility of his teaching.

Adopting time blocking transformed not only how Alex managed his time but also how he viewed his capabilities and potential. This strict yet flexible method allowed him to finally conquer a project that had seemed insurmountable for years, proving that with the right time management strategies, even the most delayed dreams can be achieved.

Tailoring Strategies to Work Preferences: Collaborative vs. Solo Workers

Procrastination can be influenced by your preferred work style. Some people thrive in collaborative settings, while others are more productive working solo. Understanding how you work best can help you manage procrastination more effectively. Let's look at two examples: Emily, who flourishes in collaborative environments, and Richard, who excels when working independently.

Collaborative Workers: Emily's Story

Emily is a 38-year-old event planner who works for a large non-profit organisation. Throughout her career, she has always thrived on teamwork and interpersonal interactions. Since her job requires organising large-scale events with multiple vendors, volunteers, and sponsors, collaboration is at the heart of her role. Emily loves bouncing ideas off others, and she finds that having a team helps her stay organised and motivated.

However, during the pandemic, when her team began working remotely, Emily noticed a significant drop in her productivity. Without the daily in-person meetings and collaborative sessions that she relied on, she started procrastinating on tasks like contacting vendors and finalising event logistics. The isolation of working alone made her feel disconnected, which in turn led to delays in her work.

Emily realised that her procrastination stemmed from her need for social interaction and team engagement to stay on track. To overcome this, she took proactive steps by setting up virtual brainstorming sessions with her team. She also initiated weekly check-ins to share progress and get feedback, ensuring that she stayed accountable. By recreating the collaborative environment virtually, Emily regained her motivation and was able to meet her deadlines without the stress of last-minute rushes.

For people like Emily, who thrive on collaboration, having systems in place for regular team interaction—whether virtual or in-person—can be key to overcoming procrastination. Setting up group calls, shared accountability measures, or working on projects together can help collaborative workers maintain productivity and avoid procrastination.

Solo Workers: Richard's Story

Richard, a 45-year-old landscape photographer, has always preferred working alone. Growing up, he was an introvert who enjoyed solitary activities like hiking, reading, and capturing nature through his camera. As an adult, he turned his passion for photography into a successful career, travelling to remote locations to capture landscapes for art galleries and private clients.

Richard's career is largely independent, and he is his own boss. While this freedom appeals to him, it also comes with challenges. Without the structure of a traditional job, Richard found himself procrastinating on post-production tasks, such as editing photos and submitting work to clients. The solitude of his job, while creatively fulfilling, sometimes led to a lack of urgency, allowing deadlines to slip.

To combat this, Richard introduced structure into his workflow by adopting the deep work method. He set specific hours each day where he would focus solely on editing and photo selection, with all distractions turned off. He also created an organised workflow for himself, scheduling editing days immediately after shooting sessions to avoid delays. Richard found that these time-blocking techniques, along with a dedicated workspace, helped him stay on top of his tasks and avoid procrastination.

For solo workers like Richard, creating personal routines and boundaries is essential to managing procrastination. Whether through time-blocking, structured work sessions, or setting up an uninterrupted workspace, independent workers can thrive by creating their own systems of accountability.

Daily Progress

By integrating these practical strategies into your daily routine, you can significantly reduce procrastination. Each method not only helps in managing tasks more effectively but also builds a framework that promotes productivity and satisfaction. As you implement these strategies, remember that the goal is not perfection but progress. Every step forward is a step away from the habit of procrastination and toward a more proactive and fulfilling life.

Reflective Questions:

- Are you setting realistic, achievable goals? How could breaking tasks into smaller steps help you stay motivated?

- Which productivity technique (breaking tasks down into smaller steps, setting mini-deadlines, or organising tasks with prioritisation) resonates with you the most?

Actionable Takeaways:

- Choose a project that you've been delaying and break it down into smaller tasks with set deadlines. Aim to complete one small step every day.

Challenge:

Choose a task you've been putting off and break it down into at least three smaller steps. Set **mini-deadlines** for each step, and use a calendar or reminders to track your progress. Complete just the first step this week. Celebrate the small win once you achieve it.

Creating a Productive Environment

Several years ago, I learned a critical lesson about the importance of minimising distractions to overcome procrastination. As the Managing Director of a busy IT firm, I had always maintained an open-door policy. This approach was intended to foster an environment where staff felt supported and could easily seek guidance on any issue. While the policy helped build a supportive team dynamic, it inadvertently became a significant source of distraction for both myself and my team members.

Whenever I faced a task that I was particularly inclined to procrastinate on, the smallest interruption, such as a team member's "quick question," could easily derail my focus. I had unknowingly perfected the art of extending these brief interruptions into lengthy discussions. This not only consumed a considerable portion of my productive time but also affected the efficiency of my colleagues, who were caught up in these extended conversations.

The turning point came when I realised that these interruptions were not just minor setbacks but a deep-seated trigger of procrastination that affected the entire team's output. Determined to address this, I devised a simple yet effective strategy: I began alternating my workdays between home and the office. On days when I was in the office, I introduced a new rule—a 'do not disturb' sign on my office door.

The sign wasn't just a barrier; it was a communication tool. It clearly indicated that I was not to be disturbed until a specified time, after which I was available for discussions, questions, and assistance. This straightforward change had a profound impact. It created a structured time for focus that was free from interruptions, allowing me to engage deeply with my work, including the tasks I tended to avoid.

The results were immediate and significant. My productivity soared as I was able to make substantial progress on projects that had been stagnant. The quality of my work improved due to the undivided attention I could give to each task. Equally important, the team adapted to this new arrangement positively. Knowing my available times, they began to organise their queries and discussions more efficiently. They also started respecting each other's focused work time more, which led to an overall increase in productivity across the company.

This experience taught me an invaluable lesson about setting boundaries and the importance of creating an environment conducive to concentration. The 'do not disturb' sign was a small change that brought about a significant shift in our office dynamics, turning previously fragmented workdays into models of efficiency and focus.

Transforming your environment into a productivity powerhouse is essential for conquering procrastination. This chapter explores strategies to minimise distractions, optimise your workspace, and enhance both physical and mental health to support efficient and focused work habits.

Minimising Distractions

One of the foremost challenges in building a more productive environment is managing distractions. These are not just minor annoyances; distractions are the primary adversaries of focus and efficiency, fragmenting your attention and significantly draining your energy. A proactive approach is necessary to reclaim your focus and escape the procrastination trap.

Simplifying Decisions to Reduce Fatigue

Mark Zuckerberg, founder of Facebook, and former U.S. President Barack Obama both manage incredibly demanding schedules. They are required to make countless critical decisions every day, from high-level strategic choices to smaller operational ones. To conserve their mental energy for the most important decisions, they've adopted a practice that may seem simple but has profound effects: they wear the same type of outfit every day. For Zuckerberg, it's a grey T-shirt, and for Obama, it was a blue or grey suit during his presidency.

This routine eliminates the need to make trivial daily decisions like what to wear, conserving mental energy for more significant matters. Psychologists refer to this phenomenon as *decision fatigue*—the idea that the quality of our decisions deteriorates after making many of them throughout the day. As renowned psychologist Roy Baumeister, co-author of *Willpower: Rediscovering the Greatest Human Strength*, explains, "Making decisions uses the very same willpower that you use to say no to doughnuts, drugs, or illicit temptations."

By simplifying daily choices, like reducing the number of decisions about clothing or routine tasks, both Zuckerberg and Obama avoid unnecessary drains on their willpower and focus. This practice is something anyone can adopt to preserve mental energy for the tasks that truly matter.

Identify Your Distractions

The first crucial step in combating distractions is to identify them clearly. Over the next week, maintain a log of what interrupts your workflow. Be specific—note whether it's a social media notification, an email alert, background noise, or interruptions from colleagues or family members. Tracking and categorising these distractions will help you understand their sources and patterns.

Understanding your personal distraction triggers allows you to develop targeted strategies to mitigate them effectively. For instance, if you find that social media consistently lures your attention away from work, that's a clear sign of where to focus your initial efforts.

Create a Distraction Plan

Once you've identified your primary distractions, the next step is to implement strategies to minimise or eliminate these interruptions. Tailor your approach to the specific distractions you face:

- For digital distractions, consider using website blockers or productivity apps that limit your access to distracting sites during work hours. Tools like Freedom or Cold Turkey can be particularly effective.

- For phone interruptions, setting your device to "Do Not Disturb" mode during critical focus times can shield you from unnecessary distractions.

- For environmental and social interruptions, such as noise from coworkers or household members, consider using noise-cancelling headphones or setting clear boundaries. Informing others of your focused work times can help establish these boundaries effectively.

Organise Your Digital Space

A cluttered digital workspace can be just as distracting as a cluttered physical workspace. Take the time to organise your digital files and keep your desktop and browser tidy:

- Organise files into clearly marked folders and regularly archive old files that are no longer immediately needed.

- Keep only essential tabs and applications open on your computer. Each additional open tab or program can invite procrastination.

By effectively identifying distractions, creating a tailored plan to minimise them, and maintaining an organised digital workspace, you can significantly enhance your ability to focus. Remember, the goal isn't to create a sterile work environment but to cultivate a space where your attention can flourish, free from the constant pull of distractions. This proactive approach not only improves productivity but also contributes to a more enjoyable and engaging work experience.

Optimising Your Workspace

Emma, a freelance illustrator, had a small desk in the corner of her one-bedroom apartment that served as her studio. Over time, the space had become cluttered with art supplies, stacks of paper, and unfinished projects. The chaos of her workspace began to mirror the chaos in her mind, leading to procrastination and a noticeable dip in her productivity and creativity.

One day, after missing a crucial deadline for the first time in her career, Emma realised the state of her workspace was a significant part of the problem. Determined to change, she decided to transform her cluttered desk into an organised, inspiring environment.

She began by clearing everything off the desk and sorting through the piles of papers and supplies. Emma invested in storage solutions: she bought a small filing cabinet for her papers, used decorative containers for her art supplies, and added a couple of shelves above her desk to organise her books and reference materials. She also invested in a better lighting solution, replacing the dim lamp with a brighter, adjustable desk lamp to reduce eye strain.

Once her desk was organised, Emma added personal touches that reflected her artistic style. She placed a few potted plants around her workspace, hung up a bulletin board for inspirational images and notes, and chose a vibrant, colourful mat for her desk chair.

The transformation was more than just physical. With a clean and orderly space, Emma found it easier to start her projects and stay focused. Her new workspace boosted her motivation; she felt more professional and in control of her work. The clear separation of materials and tools allowed her to streamline her workflow, reducing the time spent searching for the right pen or paper. This efficiency significantly decreased her tendency to procrastinate because she was no longer overwhelmed by her environment.

Emma's experience illustrates how transforming a physical space can lead to profound changes in work habits. By creating a vibrant and orderly workspace, she not only enhanced her efficiency but also rediscovered her joy in illustration, which had been stifled under the clutter and chaos of her previous setup.

Creating an environment conducive to productivity involves more than just organisation—it requires a thoughtful setup that enhances both comfort and focus. The physical and aesthetic aspects of your workspace can significantly impact your ability to concentrate and your overall inclination to procrastinate. Let's explore how optimising your workspace can lead to enhanced productivity.

Ergonomic Setup

The comfort of your workspace is paramount. An ergonomic setup not only prevents physical strain and potential injuries but also promotes longer periods of concentration. Here's how you can achieve an ergonomic workspace:

- Choose the right chair and desk: Ensure that your chair supports your back comfortably and your desk is at a suitable height to prevent hunching or straining. Your feet should rest flat on the floor, and your computer screen should be at eye level to avoid neck strain.

- Lighting is crucial: Good lighting reduces eye strain and fatigue. If possible, position your desk to benefit from natural light, but make sure there is no glare on your screen. Supplement with soft, ambient lighting that adequately illuminates your workspace without creating harsh contrasts.

- Minimise clutter: Keep your workspace tidy and organised. A cluttered desk can distract you and impede your ability to find necessary materials, which can lead to frustration and procrastination.

Change Your Scenery

Sometimes, a change in environment can significantly refresh your mind and boost your productivity. If you have the option, try to alternate workspaces. For instance:

- If you work from home, consider setting up separate areas for different types of work: one for deep-focus tasks and another for lighter administrative tasks.

- If changing rooms isn't an option, even rearranging your current setup can provide a new perspective and invigorate your workspace.

- Occasionally, working from a public space like a library or a café can provide a burst of motivation from the new surroundings and the presence of others engaged in their work.

Personalise Your Space

Personal touches can transform your workspace from a generic area into a personalised haven that inspires and motivates you:

- Incorporate plants: Adding greenery can beautify your space and improve air quality, making your environment more pleasant and conducive to work.

- Display motivational elements: Whether it's art, quotes that inspire you, or personal mementoes that remind you of your goals, these items can provide motivation and a personal connection to your workspace.

- Choose accessories that inspire: Colourful organisers, stylish stationery, or a unique keyboard can make everyday tools feel more personal and enjoyable to use.

An optimised workspace is a powerful tool in the battle against procrastination. By ensuring ergonomic comfort, changing your scenery occasionally, and infusing personal elements into your space, you create an environment that not only supports your physical well-being but also promotes mental clarity and motivation. Remember, the goal is to make your workspace a place where you not only have to be but want to be. This alignment of functionality and personalisation fosters a productive atmosphere where work becomes both effective and enjoyable.

Physical and Mental Health

Michael, a software engineer, found himself in a rut. Long hours in front of the computer, chronic stress, and an erratic work schedule had led to weight gain, poor sleep, and an overwhelming sense of burnout. His mental fog and lack of energy weren't just affecting his health; they were also leading him to procrastinate on important projects, causing further anxiety and job dissatisfaction.

The cycle of procrastination and stress continued until a routine check-up revealed alarming news about his health. Realising he needed to make a change not just for his career but also for his long-term well-being, Michael decided to take action.

He started by introducing regular exercise into his daily routine. Instead of trying sporadic intense workouts, which he knew he'd likely skip, he chose a more manageable approach: a 30-minute walk every morning before work. This simple activity not only improved his physical health but also cleared his mind and prepared him for the day ahead.

Alongside physical exercise, Michael began practising mindfulness. He started with just five minutes a day, using a guided meditation app every evening. Gradually, as he became more comfortable with the practice, he increased the duration. These mindfulness sessions helped him develop a greater awareness of his thoughts and feelings, reducing his impulse to procrastinate when faced with daunting tasks.

The changes in his routine had a profound effect. The morning walks gave Michael a burst of energy and a sense of accomplishment that carried over into his workday. He noticed that he started projects with more enthusiasm and sustained focus, significantly cutting down on his procrastination. The evening meditation sessions, meanwhile, helped him unwind and improved his sleep quality, which further enhanced his productivity and mood the following day.

Michael's integration of exercise and mindfulness into his daily life not only helped him overcome his chronic procrastination but also transformed his overall well-being. His story is a testament to the power of a holistic approach to tackling procrastination, demonstrating that sometimes, boosting productivity starts with taking better care of oneself.

The correlation between your physical and mental health and your productivity cannot be overstated. A strong body and a clear, focused mind are your greatest assets in combating procrastination. By nurturing both, you create an internal environment that supports diligence and efficiency. Here's how you can foster physical and mental well-being to enhance your productivity.

Regular Exercise

Incorporating regular exercise into your daily routine is beneficial for maintaining physical fitness and crucial for enhancing mental clarity and productivity. Consistent physical activity can transform your well-being and day-to-day efficiency.

Boosts Energy Levels

Regular exercise significantly enhances overall energy levels, bolstering physical stamina and mental alertness. Scientific research supports the impact of engaging in physical activity, particularly at strategic times such as in the morning or during work breaks.

- Morning Exercise for Increased Vigour: A study by Puetz, T. W., Flowers, S. S., & O'Connor, P. J. (2008) in the *Psychotherapy and Psychosomatics* journal found that engaging in aerobic exercise significantly boosts feelings of energy in sedentary young adults, suggesting that starting the day with physical activity can lead to sustained energy levels throughout the day.

- Benefits of High-Intensity Interval Training (HIIT): Research by Boutcher (2011) in the *Journal of Obesity* shows that HIIT not only helps with fat loss but also significantly increases metabolic rate. This type of exercise, involving short bursts of intense activity, can quickly elevate energy levels and is ideal for incorporating into work breaks to rejuvenate the mind and body.

- Long-term Benefits of Regular Physical Activity: Puetz (2006) in *Sports Medicine* provides extensive evidence that regular physical activity correlates with improved energy levels across various demographics. This longitudinal perspective supports the role of consistent exercise in maintaining high energy levels over time.

Incorporating activities like brisk walking, cycling, or HIIT into your daily routine can dramatically increase your energy, making you more equipped to tackle daily tasks with vigour and endurance. This isn't just beneficial for your physical health but is also crucial in sustaining mental energy and focus, critical for productivity and performance in professional and personal settings.

Enhances Brain Function

Aerobic exercises, such as jogging, swimming, or even dancing, increase your heart rate, which in turn boosts the circulation of blood and oxygen to your brain. This enhanced blood flow contributes to improved brain function, particularly in areas related to memory and cognitive flexibility. According to a study by Hayes et al. (2014) in the *Journal of Psychiatric Research*, exercise can improve cognitive functions and mood, which are essential for mental alertness. This study indicates that exercise, especially in the morning, primes the brain for enhanced performance throughout the day. Over time, regular exercise can lead to better problem-solving skills, enhanced memory, and quicker learning abilities. By improving brain health, physical activity supports sharper thinking and more effective decision-making, both critical components in managing daily tasks and long-term projects.

Reduces Stress

Exercise is a powerful stress reliever. It stimulates the production of endorphins, often known as the body's natural painkillers and mood elevators. These brain chemicals play an essential role in reducing stress levels, which is crucial for maintaining focus and productivity. Exercise helps clear your mind by lowering stress, making it easier to concentrate on tasks without the cloud of anxiety or tension. Whether it's a session of yoga, a swim, or a simple stretching routine, regular physical activity can help keep stress at bay, fostering a more relaxed, productive mindset.

Making Exercise a Pleasurable Habit

To truly reap the benefits of exercise, it's important to choose activities that you enjoy. This makes it more likely that you will stick to a regular exercise regimen. Whether it's a morning jog that clears your mind, a yoga session that relaxes you, or a cycling trip that energises you, finding pleasure in your fitness activities ensures that exercise is a welcomed and sustainable part of your lifestyle. Setting realistic goals, tracking your progress, and perhaps partnering with a friend for joint workouts can also enhance your motivation and enjoyment.

Regular exercise is a cornerstone of not just physical health, but mental and emotional well-being, playing a crucial role in enhancing productivity and mental clarity. By integrating physical activity into your daily routine, you not only boost your physical stamina and mental acuity but also manage stress more effectively and enhance your overall brain function. Start small, find activities that engage and excite you, and build from there. As you make exercise a regular part of your life, you'll likely notice significant improvements in your ability to focus, solve problems, and handle the challenges of daily life with resilience and vigour.

Mindfulness and Relaxation

Mindfulness and relaxation techniques are invaluable tools for maintaining mental health and enhancing cognitive focus, which are crucial for effectively managing and overcoming procrastination. By incorporating these practices into your daily routine, you can significantly reduce stress, alleviate anxiety, and achieve a clearer state of mind, thus boosting your productivity and overall well-being.

Mindfulness Meditation

Mindfulness meditation is a practice that involves focusing your attention on the present moment, often through simple actions like observing your breath or a specific object. This technique helps centre your thoughts and prevents them from overwhelming you, which is essential for maintaining mental clarity. A study published in the journal *Mindfulness* found that regular mindfulness meditation can significantly reduce symptoms of anxiety and depression, and enhance attention and concentration (Creswell, J.D., et al., 2014).

Begin with just five minutes of mindfulness meditation each day. You can gradually increase the duration as you become more comfortable with the practice. Use apps or guided sessions if you find it difficult to maintain focus on your own.

Progressive Muscle Relaxation

Progressive Muscle Relaxation (PMR) is a technique that involves tensing and then relaxing each muscle group in your body. This process helps to identify areas of tension and release it, contributing to overall physical relaxation and stress relief. Research has shown that PMR can be effective in reducing physiological symptoms of stress and can also help in reducing general anxiety (Conrad, A., & Roth, W.T., 2007).

Start by tensing the muscles in your toes for five seconds, then relax them for 30 seconds, and gradually work your way up through each muscle group to your neck and head. Practice PMR in a quiet, comfortable spot where you can sit or lie down without interruption. This can be especially beneficial before bedtime or during a break in your workday.

Deep Breathing Exercises

Deep breathing exercises are a simple yet powerful way to restore a balanced mental state, particularly useful in high-pressure environments. By focusing on deep, controlled breathing, you can slow your heart rate and lower blood pressure, creating a feeling of calmness that can help clear your mind. Studies have demonstrated that deep breathing can have an immediate effect on diffusing emotional stress and anxiety, which are often precursors to procrastination (Ma, X., et al., 2017).

Try the 4-7-8 breathing technique, which involves breathing in deeply for four seconds, holding the breath for seven seconds, and exhaling slowly for eight seconds. This method can be practised almost anywhere and is particularly effective during work breaks or moments when you feel overwhelmed.

Incorporating mindfulness and relaxation techniques such as mindfulness meditation, progressive muscle relaxation, and deep breathing exercises into your daily routine can be transformative. These practices not only help in managing stress and anxiety but also enhance your ability to focus and maintain clarity of thought, directly combating the mental and emotional blocks that lead to procrastination. By dedicating a few minutes each day to these techniques, you can significantly improve your mental health and boost your productivity, paving the way for a more focused and balanced life.

Healthy Lifestyle Choices

The pivotal role that adequate sleep and a balanced diet play in maintaining productivity cannot be overstated. These fundamental elements of a healthy lifestyle are crucial not only for physical health but also for optimal mental functioning. Integrating these practices effectively can help reduce procrastination by improving your overall energy levels, focus, and cognitive function.

Adequate Sleep

Sleep is a critical component of mental and physical health. Regular, quality sleep—typically 7-9 hours per night for adults—ensures that the brain functions at its best. Insufficient sleep has been linked to reduced attention span, worsened memory, and slower cognitive processing, all of which can contribute to increased procrastination. According to a study by Alhola and Polo-Kantola (2007), sleep deprivation impairs cognitive and motor performance in a way similar to alcohol intoxication. Ensuring adequate sleep is, therefore, essential for maintaining clarity of thought and the ability to manage tasks efficiently.

Establish a consistent sleep schedule by going to bed and waking up at the same time every day, even on weekends. Create a bedtime routine that promotes relaxation, such as reading a book or taking a warm bath, to enhance the quality of your sleep.

Balanced Diet

Eating a nutritious, balanced diet is equally important for cognitive function and energy levels. Foods rich in omega-3 fatty acids, antioxidants, and vitamins play a direct role in brain health, influencing everything from mood regulation to memory and decision-making. Incorporate foods like oily fish (e.g., salmon, mackerel), nuts (e.g., walnuts, almonds), seeds (e.g., flaxseeds, chia seeds), yoghurt, and blueberries into your diet. These foods are known for their beneficial effects on brain health. Gómez-Pinilla, in a 2008 study, highlighted that the omega-3 fatty acids found in fish oil are critical for optimal brain function. Additionally, antioxidants from berries are known to reduce oxidative stress and inflammation in the brain, which can enhance cognitive processing.

Plan meals that include a variety of nutrients, focusing on incorporating fresh fruits, vegetables, lean proteins, and whole grains. Preparing meals in advance can help ensure you maintain a balanced diet, even on busy days.

By prioritising sleep and nutrition, you are not only boosting your day-to-day productivity but also investing in your long-term health and well-being. These healthy lifestyle choices lay a strong foundation for a resilient body and mind, enabling you to approach daily tasks with increased vigour and a clearer mind. Regular exercise, mindfulness practices, and maintaining these fundamental health practices are your best defence against the pitfalls of procrastination. Remember, a well-rested, well-nourished body is equipped to perform at its best, making it easier to stay focused and efficient in all your endeavours.

Three Pronged Attack

Creating a productive environment involves more than just physical space—it encompasses managing distractions, optimising your workspace, and maintaining your health. By taking control of these aspects, you can create a setting that not only encourages productivity but also supports your overall well-being and success.

Reflective Questions:

- How does your current workspace contribute to or hinder your productivity?

- What specific distractions are preventing you from focusing on your tasks?

Actionable Takeaways:

- Identify three distractions in your workspace. Eliminate or minimise them immediately. Try decluttering your desk or creating a clear boundary between work and relaxation areas.

Challenge:

This week, reorganise your workspace. Clean up any clutter, add an element of inspiration (e.g., artwork, plants), and create a workspace that encourages focus and minimises distractions.

Advanced Techniques and Tools

Once the foundational strategies to combat procrastination are in place, it's time to elevate your productivity with advanced techniques and tools. This chapter explores how leveraging technology, establishing accountability systems, and implementing reward systems can further enhance your ability to manage time and tasks effectively.

Using Technology Wisely

In today's digital age, technology is not just a part of our daily lives; it shapes the way we work, think, and interact. When used strategically, technology can be a formidable ally in the battle against procrastination, enhancing productivity and fostering effective work habits.

Tom, a project manager at a mid-sized marketing agency, struggled with keeping track of multiple campaigns, deadlines, and team responsibilities. His approach had always been somewhat old-school, relying on handwritten notes and memory. However, as the scope and number of projects grew, this method led to missed deadlines, forgotten tasks, and an overwhelming sense of chaos. Procrastination became Tom's unintended response to this overwhelming workload, as he found himself unsure of what to tackle next.

Realising he needed a change to salvage his productivity and reduce his stress, Tom decided to embrace technology by integrating a task management app into his daily routine. After some research, he chose Asana, attracted by its user-friendly interface and robust feature set.

Tom started by inputting all current and upcoming projects into Asana, breaking them down into tasks and subtasks. He assigned each task a deadline and designated team members responsible for each one. The app allowed him to visualise the entire workflow of multiple projects simultaneously, which helped him prioritise tasks more effectively.

The immediate impact of using Asana was a clearer mind and a more organised approach to his day. Every morning, Tom reviewed his tasks for the day, adjusting priorities as needed right from the app. The ability to see everything laid out clearly helped reduce his anxiety about what to do next, which had often led to procrastination.

Moreover, the app's reminder and follow-up features ensured that nothing fell through the cracks. Tom could set reminders for himself and also automate follow-ups with team members, ensuring that projects stayed on track without him needing to keep everything in his head or continually chase people down.

As weeks turned into months, Tom's newfound organisational skills earned him recognition at his agency. Projects were completed on time more consistently, team productivity soared, and Tom's career took a positive turn. He found himself less likely to procrastinate, not only because he was more organised but also because the anxiety that once triggered his procrastination was greatly diminished.

Tom's story illustrates the transformative power of integrating task management technology into daily work routines. By embracing this tool, he dramatically enhanced his project management skills, streamlined workflows, and cut down significantly on procrastination, leading to a more rewarding and less stressful professional life.

Task Management Apps

Task management applications are essential tools for anyone looking to streamline their workflow and enhance efficiency. Platforms like Trello, Asana, or Todoist offer robust functionalities that help you organise tasks into projects, set specific deadlines, and monitor progress in real time. These tools allow for a high degree of customisation, enabling you to tailor the app's functionality to suit your specific needs, whether you're managing a complex team project or organising personal tasks.

One key benefit of these apps is their ability to synchronise across all your devices, ensuring you can access your tasks and schedules whether you're at your desk or on the go. This seamless integration helps maintain a continuous flow of work, reducing downtime and keeping you consistently productive.

Focus Enhancers

Maintaining focus in an environment teeming with distractions can be challenging. Focus-enhancing apps, such as Forest, provide innovative solutions to this problem. Forest rewards users with virtual trees that grow as you concentrate on your tasks. This gamified approach not only helps you stay focused but also builds a visually rewarding representation of your dedication and hard work.

As my daughter geared up for her GCSE exams, she was determined to eliminate procrastination and minimize distractions. Aware of the challenges posed by smartphones and social media, she decided to leverage technology in a way that would enhance her study efficiency rather than detract from it. She discovered the Flora app, a focus enhancer designed to help users maintain concentration by minimizing phone-related distractions.

The Flora app operates on a simple yet effective principle: it blocks notifications from messaging, news, and social media apps for a designated study period. If the user stays off their phone for the duration of this period, they are rewarded with badges and the virtual growth of a forest within the app. This gamification adds a layer of motivation that is both fun and rewarding. Additionally, the app offers an option to contribute financially to real-world forestry projects, intertwining personal productivity with a greater environmental cause.

My daughter diligently used the Flora app throughout her exam preparation period. She would set the app to run during her study sessions, committing to not use her phone until her study timer ended. Often I would call her for a meal or some other reason only to be told "I still have 10 minutes on my study timer". This routine helped her build a disciplined study schedule, free from the interruptions that typically plague students in the digital era.

Over the course of her revision, she accumulated over 600 hours of focused study time, earned multiple badges, and enjoyed the satisfaction of growing various virtual forests. But the real reward came in the form of her exam results—she achieved top marks in most of her subjects, particularly in those where she devoted the most focused study time using the app.

My daughter's experience highlights the potential of focus-enhancing apps like Flora to transform students' study habits and academic performance. By effectively blocking out distractions and creating a reward system for maintaining focus, my daughter was able to devote her full attention to her studies, leading to exemplary academic achievements. For students struggling with distraction, incorporating such a tool can be a game-changer, not only during exam season but in any endeavour that requires deep focus and commitment.

For those who need a more stringent approach to managing distractions, applications like Freedom or Cold Turkey allow you to block distracting websites and applications during designated times. By restricting access to potential distractions, these tools help you maintain focus on the task at hand, effectively reducing procrastination and boosting productivity.

Time Tracking Tools

Understanding how you spend your time is crucial for effective time management. Time-tracking tools such as RescueTime or Toggl offer insightful analytics into your daily activities, allowing you to identify productivity patterns and pinpoint time-consuming activities that do not add significant value. These tools run quietly in the background, compiling data on how much time you spend on various tasks throughout the day.

With this information, you can make informed decisions about how to structure your day for maximum efficiency. For instance, if you notice that you're most productive in the morning hours, you can schedule your most demanding tasks for this time. Conversely, identifying times when you're prone to procrastination can help you plan breaks or less intensive activities, keeping your day balanced and productive.

Leveraging technology wisely means choosing tools that complement your work style and enhance your productivity. By integrating task management apps, focus enhancers, and time-tracking tools into your routine, you harness the power of technology to create a disciplined, efficient, and highly productive work environment. Embrace these technologies not as crutches, but as catalysts that propel you toward your goals, minimising procrastination and maximising your potential.

Accountability Systems

Accountability systems are a cornerstone of effective time management and productivity enhancement. By creating a structure of accountability, you can significantly amplify your commitment to tasks, making it less tempting to procrastinate. These systems provide an external check that can motivate you to maintain progress and meet deadlines.

Accountability Partners

A few years ago, I found myself confronting a reality that many face: my lifestyle had become increasingly sedentary, and my fitness levels were alarmingly low. Despite initial efforts to enhance my fitness, my routine lacked consistency, and the results were far from satisfactory. As time passed, my motivation dwindled, and procrastination became my response to scheduled runs or gym sessions, leading me back to the sedentary lifestyle I had vowed to change.

Realising a need for a drastic change in strategy, I turned to the concept of accountability partners by joining a group fitness boot camp that met every Saturday morning. This decision marked the beginning of a transformative journey in my health and fitness life.

The group dynamic at the boot camp provided not just encouragement but a robust system of accountability. The camaraderie and collective energy of the group made each session more engaging and less of a chore. Every week, we committed to not only participating in the workouts but also motivating each other to achieve our personal best. This supportive environment was pivotal; it was about more than just exercising together—it was a commitment to each other's success.

As the weeks turned into months, our interactions evolved into regular check-ins. We held each other accountable for runs between classes and additional sessions at the gym. This ongoing encouragement played a crucial role in maintaining my routine, pushing me to stay on track even when my motivation was low. Over time, this consistent effort led to significant improvements in my fitness levels.

After a year of regular boot camp sessions and consistent personal workouts, my fitness improved to the point where I felt confident enough to enrol in a cross-country race with obstacles.

Though I didn't finish with a leading time, I placed in the top half of participants in my age group—a milestone that seemed unattainable just a year prior. Buoyed by this achievement and the relentless support of my boot camp colleagues, I tackled an even more daunting challenge: the "Tough Mudder" half marathon, a gruelling course designed by special forces to test the fittest and most determined enthusiasts. At the age of 50, I completed this challenge, not with speed, but with the tenacity and resilience fostered by my accountability group.

This journey wasn't just about the physical challenges; it was a transformative experience that reshaped my approach to health and fitness. Even today, 11 years later, I continue to annually participate with the same accountability partners in fitness challenges that keep us committed to our health. The enduring power of accountability has not only helped me achieve goals that once seemed unreachable but has also instilled a lifelong commitment to fitness.

Having an accountability partner is one of the most direct and personal ways to ensure you stay on track. This partner could be a colleague, friend, or coach—someone who is reliable and willing to check in on your progress regularly. The key to this relationship is regular communication. Whether it's a brief daily update or a more detailed weekly review, these check-ins can motivate you to accomplish what you've committed to, knowing someone else is aware of your goals and progress.

An effective accountability partner is someone who is not afraid to challenge you if you start to slip or procrastinate. They should encourage you and push you to maintain your commitments. This dynamic can significantly boost your motivation and drive to complete tasks, particularly during periods when your motivation might wane.

Group Accountability

Joining or forming a group with similar goals can harness the power of community to foster accountability. Group settings create a network of support and motivation that is hard to replicate in solitary settings. Regular meetings allow you to share your progress, celebrate successes, and discuss challenges. This not only keeps you accountable but also provides a platform for receiving constructive feedback and learning from others' experiences.

Group accountability can be particularly effective because it taps into our natural desire for belonging and approval. The group serves as a constant reminder of your commitments, and the expectations of your peers can spur you to action. Additionally, seeing others achieve their goals can be a powerful motivator to match their progress.

Digital Accountability

Jessica, a freelance writer, had always dreamed of writing a novel. Over the years, she started numerous manuscripts but struggled to see any of them through to completion. The solitary nature of writing made it easy for her to put off work for days or even weeks, with no immediate repercussions other than her growing frustration and disappointment.

After another year passed without significant progress, Jessica knew she needed a change if she was ever going to finish her novel. She reached out to a former writing classmate, Derek, who faced similar challenges. They agreed to become accountability partners, setting up a system where they would meet weekly to discuss their progress, challenges, and next steps.

These accountability meetings quickly became a cornerstone of Jessica's writing process. Each week, she and Derek shared what they had accomplished, provided feedback on each other's work, and set goals for the next week. Knowing she had to report her progress to Derek provided Jessica with the external motivation she needed to sit down and write regularly. The meetings also offered a space for discussing problems and brainstorming solutions, reducing the feeling of isolation that often overwhelmed her during the writing process. Whenever Jessica felt stuck or demotivated, Derek was there to offer support and encouragement, reminding her of the reasons she started writing in the first place.

As months passed, Jessica found that her procrastination decreased significantly. The regular rhythm of the meetings created a structure that helped her manage her time and tasks more effectively. She no longer waited until she felt inspired to write; instead, she developed a steady, disciplined approach to her work. Ultimately, the support and accountability system paid off. Jessica completed her novel—a goal she had been chasing for over five years. The novel was not only a personal triumph but also marked the beginning of a more disciplined and productive phase of her career. Jessica credits the accountability system with transforming her approach to writing and helping her achieve a dream that once seemed unreachable.

Jessica's story highlights the power of accountability in overcoming procrastination. Regular check-ins and mutual support can provide the external motivation and feedback necessary to stay committed to long-term goals, especially when progress is slow and the temptation to abandon the project is high.

In the digital age, technology offers additional layers of accountability. Utilising digital platforms where you must report progress can keep you accountable not only to yourself but also to others. Tools like project management software are excellent for this purpose. They allow you to post updates, track progress, and even integrate feedback from team members or coaches. These platforms are particularly useful in professional settings where multiple stakeholders are involved.

Digital accountability tools often provide visual progress indicators, which can be incredibly motivating. They allow you to see at a glance how far you've come and how much closer you are to achieving your goals. This can be a compelling incentive to keep pushing forward, minimising procrastination.

Implementing robust accountability systems can transform your approach to work and personal projects. Whether through partnerships, groups, or digital tools, these systems provide the structure and motivation necessary to propel you towards your goals. Embrace accountability as a means to enhance your productivity and as a strategy to combat the allure of procrastination. By holding yourself accountable, you not only improve your chances of success but also set a pattern of disciplined, purposeful work habits that can last a lifetime.

Reward Systems

Alan, a software developer, had always struggled with procrastination, especially when it came to personal projects. One of his long-standing goals was to develop an independent app—a side project that he was passionate about but kept pushing aside due to his demanding job and tendency to delay tasks that lacked immediate deadlines.

Determined to break this cycle of procrastination, Alan decided to implement a reward system to motivate progress and completion of his app. He structured the rewards to cater to both small milestones and major achievements, aiming to keep his motivation high throughout the development process.

For small milestones, such as completing the app's wireframe or finishing the code for a key feature, Alan rewarded himself with immediate, enjoyable treats. These included things like a favourite coffee from a local café or an evening watching a movie. These small rewards provided immediate satisfaction after reaching a mini-goal, making the work feel more gratifying and less like a chore.

For larger milestones, like completing the beta version of the app or successfully testing it, Alan set up more significant rewards. These included a weekend getaway or purchasing a gadget he had wanted for a long time. These bigger rewards were crucial for keeping him focused over the long term, as they provided something substantial to look forward to.

This system of tiered rewards transformed Alan's approach to his project. The small rewards kept his daily motivation buoyant, making it easier to chip away at the project regularly. The anticipation of larger rewards helped maintain his enthusiasm for the broader scope of work, driving him to complete substantial chunks of the project to reach those higher milestones.

After months of consistent effort, Alan finally completed his app. The day he launched it on the app store, he treated himself to the biggest reward of all: a high-end new laptop he had eyed for months, which would help him with future projects. The success of his app—both in its completion and its reception— reinforced the effectiveness of his reward system.

Alan's story illustrates how well-planned rewards can significantly influence motivation and productivity. By creating a system that regularly celebrated his progress, Alan found the drive to overcome procrastination and achieve a goal that once seemed daunting.

Maintaining motivation through the ups and downs of any project, especially those that are lengthy or complex, can be challenging. Implementing a structured reward system can significantly boost your enthusiasm and sustain your momentum, turning the journey toward your goals into a rewarding experience in itself.

Small Rewards

Incorporating small rewards into your daily or weekly routines is a powerful way to maintain motivation and make progress feel gratifying. These rewards should be immediate and enjoyable, serving as a direct incentive for completing tasks or reaching short-term milestones.

For instance, allow yourself a favourite coffee break after completing a difficult task or indulge in watching an episode of your favourite show after clearing your daily to-do list. These small pleasures can act as a quick reset for your mental state, refreshing and preparing you for the next task. Importantly, they also make the process enjoyable, reinforcing your motivation to engage with your tasks consistently.

Big Rewards

For larger milestones or the completion of significant projects, setting up more substantial rewards can provide something exciting to look forward to. This could be anything from a night out with friends to celebrate, purchasing a new book, or even planning a weekend getaway.

Big rewards should feel like a celebration of your hard work and achievements, making the effort you've put in feel worthwhile. They also serve as a strong motivational tool, pushing you through tougher or less interesting phases of a project with the knowledge that there is a significant payoff waiting at the end.

Visual Progress Indicators

Visual tools such as progress bars or checklists not only help you track your progress but can also act as motivational aids. Seeing a visual representation of how far you've come can be incredibly satisfying. It's a clear, concrete reminder of your achievements and how close you are to reaching your final goal.

You can use apps that include gamified progress indicators or set up a physical board in your workspace where you can mark off completed tasks. Each act of marking progress is a mini-reward in itself, providing a regular dose of satisfaction and encouragement.

Setting up a reward system is not just about giving yourself treats; it's a strategic approach to maintaining high levels of motivation throughout the lifespan of a project. By celebrating both the small wins and the big achievements, you cultivate a positive feedback loop that keeps your spirits high and your focus sharp. Remember, the key to a successful reward system is to ensure that the rewards are meaningful to you and proportionate to the effort required. This personalised approach ensures that each step forward is enjoyable and that your journey towards your goals is as rewarding as the achievements themselves.

Conclusion

Advanced techniques and tools can refine and amplify your productivity strategies, making your efforts against procrastination more effective. By wisely using technology, enforcing accountability, and rewarding your progress, you can build a robust framework that supports sustained motivation and efficiency. As you implement these strategies, remember that consistency is key. It's not just about using the tools; it's about making them a part of your daily routine to create lasting change.

Reflective Questions:

- Which technology tools (apps, time trackers, accountability systems) can help you stay on track?

- How can you leverage accountability partners or reward systems to overcome procrastination?

Actionable Takeaways:

- Set up an accountability system. Find a friend or colleague with whom you can regularly check in about your progress, or join an online group focused on productivity.

Challenge:

Try using a free productivity app like Trello, Asana, or Todoist to organise your tasks this week. Set clear deadlines and track your progress daily to stay on top of your project.

The Role of Habit Building

The battle against procrastination is not won through isolated acts of willpower but through the consistent building and reinforcing of productive habits. This chapter explores how you can develop routines, use habit stacking to incorporate new behaviours seamlessly, and ensure these changes are sustainable in the long term.

Routine Development

Sarah, a project manager in a fast-paced tech startup, found herself constantly overwhelmed by her daily tasks. Mornings were particularly chaotic, often starting with a haphazard review of emails, which led her to jump reactively from one task to another. This lack of structure not only fueled her stress levels but also entrenched her procrastination habits, as she deferred more complex projects in favour of tackling immediate, less important tasks.

Determined to change this cycle, Sarah decided to establish a morning routine that would set a productive tone for the rest of her day. She started by waking up an hour earlier than usual, giving herself a calm window before the day's demands escalated. The first 30 minutes of her morning were dedicated to a short workout, which she found not only invigorated her physically but also cleared her mind, making her more alert and focused.

After her workout, Sarah spent 15 minutes planning her day. She reviewed her tasks, prioritised them based on urgency and importance, and scheduled blocks of time for focused work, particularly for projects she had been procrastinating on. This planning session was followed by a brief meditation to centre her thoughts and fortify her intent to stick to the day's plan.

The impact of this new routine was profound. By starting her day with exercise, Sarah activated her body and mind, shaking off any inertia that might lead to procrastination. The planning session helped her take control of her schedule, rather than letting her inbox dictate her priorities. This proactive approach significantly decreased her morning procrastination; she now tackled her most challenging tasks during her peak energy hours in the morning, which improved her productivity and reduced her overall stress.

Sarah's colleagues and supervisors noticed the change in her demeanour and output. She became known for her efficiency and her ability to deliver on complex projects that she once would have avoided. The success of her new morning routine not only enhanced her professional performance but also increased her job satisfaction and her confidence in her ability to manage her responsibilities effectively.

Sarah's story demonstrates how establishing a structured, purposeful morning routine can transform an individual's productivity and mindset, turning what used to be a source of daily stress into a wellspring of personal efficacy and professional success.

Developing a well-structured routine is a cornerstone of effective habit-building. It creates a predictable and efficient framework that reduces the need for constant decision-making, which in turn diminishes the mental exhaustion associated with starting and switching tasks. A solid routine not only helps in overcoming procrastination but also enhances overall productivity by embedding consistency into your daily life.

Setting Clear Routines

The first step in establishing a powerful routine is to set clear, specific times for different types of activities. This could mean designating the first hour of your workday to tackle high-priority tasks when your energy and concentration are at their peak. Alternatively, you might adopt the Pomodoro Technique, where work is broken down into intervals—typically 25 minutes of focused work followed by a 5-minute break. This technique helps maintain high levels of productivity without leading to burnout, making it easier to start tasks because you know a break is never too far off.

Each segment of your routine should serve a specific purpose and fit logically into your daily and weekly goals. This clarity and structure make your workload manageable and less daunting, thereby reducing the inertia that often leads to procrastination.

Consistency Is Key

The true power of a routine lies in its consistent application. When actions become regular, they transform into habits—automatic responses that require less mental effort to initiate. This consistency minimises the resistance that typically accompanies the start of a task, thereby smoothing the path to productivity.

To cultivate consistency, stick to your routine as closely as possible every day. This might require some discipline initially, especially on days when motivation wanes, but the long-term benefits—reduced procrastination, increased productivity, and a more organised approach to tasks—are well worth the effort.

Adaptability

While consistency is vital for establishing effective routines, adaptability ensures that your routine continues to serve you well as circumstances change. Life is dynamic—workloads fluctuate, personal commitments arise, and goals evolve. An adaptable routine is one that can accommodate these changes without significant disruption.

For example, if a new project requires more intensive work hours, you might need to adjust your routine to start earlier in the day or to incorporate longer blocks of focused work. Being flexible and willing to modify your routine as needed is crucial for maintaining its relevance and effectiveness, ensuring that it always supports your current priorities and challenges.

A well-crafted routine is a powerful tool against procrastination. By setting clear routines, maintaining consistency, and embracing adaptability, you create a dependable framework that supports your daily efforts. This approach not only boosts productivity but also builds a resilient work ethic that can withstand the challenges of fluctuating circumstances. As you refine your routines, you'll find that they become an integral part of a balanced, productive life, turning the daunting into the doable, day after day.

Habit Stacking

Habit stacking is a powerful strategy for building new habits by leveraging the ones you already have firmly in place. This approach significantly increases the likelihood of adherence to new behaviours by linking them to routines that are already automatic. By creating a compound effect, habit stacking can accelerate your productivity and streamline your daily routines seamlessly.

Identify Existing Habits

The first step in effective habit stacking is to identify the stable routines already embedded in your daily life. These are the habits that are so ingrained in your routine that you perform them almost without thinking. Common examples include having a morning coffee, brushing your teeth, or the routine you follow right before going to bed.

Take note of these moments throughout your day. These are your anchors—routine actions that you can use as the foundation for stacking new habits. The key is to choose habits that are well-established and occur at a consistent time and place each day, as this regularity creates the perfect setting for introducing new behaviours.

Attach New Habits

Once you have identified your anchor habits, the next step is to attach new, productive behaviours to them. The goal is to make the transition between the established habit and the new one as smooth as possible.

For instance, if your morning coffee is an established part of your routine, consider using the time immediately following this as your cue to begin a 15-minute planning session for the day's tasks. The act of finishing your coffee naturally leads to the task of planning. This method not only ensures that you remember to plan out your day but also places this new habit in a context that enhances its execution.

Gradual Integration

Simon, a content strategist at a bustling digital marketing firm, found his afternoons to be particularly challenging. After lunch, he often felt a slump in energy and focus, which led to procrastination, especially with tasks that required high cognitive effort. Despite trying various strategies to overcome this midday lull, he struggled to maintain productivity throughout the afternoon.

Determined to change this pattern, Simon decided to try habit stacking, a strategy he learned about in a productivity workshop. He already had a consistent habit of taking a short walk during his lunch break to clear his mind and stretch his legs. Deciding to build upon this existing habit, he added a 10-minute meditation session immediately after his walk, before returning to his desk.

Simon used a guided meditation app on his phone, focusing on sessions designed to enhance concentration and energy. This brief meditation provided a mental reset, allowing him to approach the afternoon's tasks with renewed focus and calm.

The effect of this new routine was noticeable almost immediately. The meditation helped mitigate the post-lunch energy dip and sharpened his focus. By stacking this new habit onto an already established one, Simon found it easy to incorporate it into his daily routine without feeling like an additional task on his to-do list.

As weeks turned into months, Simon's afternoons transformed from a productivity struggle to his most productive time of day. He no longer put off difficult tasks until the last minute but tackled them head-on with the clarity and concentration he had cultivated through his post-lunch meditation. His colleagues and supervisors took note of the change, praising his ability to produce high-quality work consistently throughout the day.

Simon's successful integration of habit stacking not only enhanced his professional performance but also significantly reduced his daily stress levels. By linking a short meditation to his existing lunchtime walk, he created a powerful routine that effectively combated his tendency to procrastinate and boosted his overall well-being.

The process of habit stacking works best when new habits are introduced gradually. Start with small, manageable changes that can be easily integrated into your existing routines. The simplicity of the new habit increases the chances that you will stick with it long enough for it to become automatic.

As these new habits begin to solidify, they themselves can become anchors for additional behaviours. Over time, you can build a complex network of interconnected habits, each supporting and reinforcing the others. This layered approach not only improves productivity but also deepens the resilience of your daily routine, making it robust against disruptions.

Habit stacking is an effective method for cultivating new productive behaviours by strategically linking them to the established routines in your life. By identifying your existing habits, attaching new ones, and integrating them gradually, you create a sustainable ecosystem of behaviours that propel you toward greater efficiency and effectiveness. This approach not only simplifies the process of adopting new habits but also ensures that they stick, providing long-term benefits to your productivity and overall well-being.

Long-Term Sustainability

Maria, an aspiring marketing executive, initially struggled with procrastination, which often hindered her career progression. Early in her career, she found that despite her hard work and talent, she wasn't achieving her goals or fulfilling her potential. This was largely due to her inconsistent productivity habits, which saw her putting off important tasks until the pressure mounted to unsustainable levels.

Determined to turn her career trajectory around, Maria began adopting various productivity techniques, such as the

Pomodoro Technique for time management and the Eisenhower Matrix for task prioritisation. While these methods brought some initial improvements, Maria knew that sustaining these changes would be the real challenge.

Over the years, Maria committed to reviewing her productivity habits every three months. During these reviews, she assessed what was working and what wasn't and adapted her strategies accordingly. For instance, she found that while the Pomodoro Technique was helpful in keeping her focused, she needed longer blocks of time for creative tasks, leading her to adjust her schedule to include extended periods of deep work.

Additionally, Maria recognised the importance of rewards in sustaining motivation. She set up a system where completing a week's worth of tasks without significant procrastination earned her a small reward, like a movie night or a favourite treat. For larger milestones, such as successfully completing a major project or achieving a quarterly goal, she rewarded herself with something more substantial, like a weekend getaway.

Her commitment to refining and maintaining her productivity habits paid off. Over the years, not only did her ability to manage and execute tasks improve, but her consistent performance led to several promotions. Eventually, she achieved her goal of becoming a marketing director, a role in which she could mentor others. Maria's journey of continual self-improvement and adaptation in her productivity habits not only advanced her career but also contributed significantly to her personal development.

Maria's story illustrates the importance of not just adopting productivity habits but also continually refining and sustaining them. Her willingness to regularly review and adjust her methods played a crucial role in her long-term success, both professionally and personally.

Ensuring that the habits you cultivate not only take root but also thrive long-term is essential to transforming your productivity and personal effectiveness. The process of building and maintaining these habits should be dynamic and adaptive, continuously evolving to meet your changing needs and circumstances.

Regular Reviews

To sustain the benefits of new habits, it's crucial to integrate regular reviews into your routine. These periodic evaluations allow you to assess the effectiveness of each habit and determine whether it still serves your goals or needs adjustment. Schedule time monthly or quarterly to reflect on your routines, considering what's working well and what might need to be changed.

During these reviews, ask yourself questions like:

- Have my goals changed since I started this habit?

- Is this habit helping me progress towards my goals?

- Do I need to increase the challenge of this habit to continue growing?

This ongoing process of assessment ensures that your habits remain relevant and aligned with your overarching objectives, making it more likely that they will endure over time.

Reward Progress

Consistently acknowledging and rewarding yourself for maintaining your new habits is vital for long-term sustainability. These rewards reinforce the positive behaviours you're developing and make the process more enjoyable and motivating.

Choose meaningful rewards that genuinely motivate you to stick to your habits. These could be anything from a small treat for daily successes to larger rewards for more significant milestones. For instance, after maintaining a new habit for a month, you might treat yourself to a day out or a new book. Celebrating these achievements helps cement the habits as valued parts of your routine.

Community Support

Incorporating a social element into your habit-building process can greatly enhance its sustainability. Sharing your goals and progress with a community or a group of like-minded individuals creates a supportive network that encourages perseverance. Whether it's an online forum, a local club, or a group of friends, being part of a community allows you to share challenges, exchange tips, and celebrate successes together.

Community support also introduces a layer of accountability, which can be incredibly motivating. Knowing that others are aware of your goals and progress can spur you to uphold your commitments. Additionally, seeing others succeed in their habit-building efforts can inspire and motivate you to continue developing your own habits.

The journey of building and sustaining new habits is ongoing and ever-evolving. By integrating regular reviews, rewarding progress, and engaging with a supportive community, you create a robust framework that fosters long-term habit sustainability. These strategies ensure that your new habits remain dynamic and adaptable, continuously contributing to your personal and professional growth. As you refine and adapt your habits over time, you solidify the changes into lasting transformations that significantly enhance your life.

Form Good Habits

Building and maintaining productive habits is a dynamic process that requires regular attention and intention. By developing effective routines, stacking new habits onto existing ones, and focusing on long-term sustainability, you can transform the landscape of your daily life, turning productivity into a natural and enjoyable part of your day.

Reflective Questions:

- What daily habits are contributing to or hindering your productivity?

- How can habit stacking (adding new habits to existing ones) help you build momentum?

Actionable Takeaways:

- Start by adding one positive habit to your daily routine. For example, after making coffee each morning, spend 10 minutes planning your day.

Challenge:

For the next 30 days, work on developing one key habit that combats procrastination, such as writing every morning or reviewing your to-do list. Track your progress and reflect on how it's impacting your productivity.

Special Topics

Procrastination is a complex behaviour influenced by a variety of factors. This chapter delves into some special topics that provide deeper insights into the nuances of procrastination, including its psychological underpinnings, the diversity of procrastination patterns, and the influence of cultural and personal differences. Understanding these elements can enhance the effectiveness of your strategies to overcome procrastination.

Addressing Underlying Issues

Hannah, a digital marketing specialist, had always prided herself on her ability to meet deadlines and manage multiple projects efficiently. However, over the past year, she noticed a significant change in her behaviour. Her usual zest for work had diminished, and she began to delay tasks, often finding herself paralysed by the simplest decisions. She also started to withdraw from her colleagues and lost interest in activities that once brought her joy.

At first, Hannah attributed her procrastination and lack of enthusiasm to burnout from her demanding job. But as her symptoms persisted, she began to wonder if something deeper was affecting her productivity and overall well-being. After several months of struggling, Hannah finally confided in a close friend who suggested that her procrastination might be linked to depression.

Taking her friend's advice to heart, Hannah sought professional help. She was initially hesitant to discuss her work problems, fearing judgement or misunderstanding, but she found a therapist who specialised in occupational stress and mental health. During therapy, Hannah learned that her procrastination was indeed a symptom of underlying depression. The realisation was both a relief and a wake-up call.

With her therapist's guidance, Hannah began a comprehensive treatment plan, including cognitive-behavioural therapy (CBT) to address her negative thought patterns and practical strategies to manage her workload more effectively. She also started medication to help manage her depressive symptoms.

As her therapy progressed, Hannah noticed a gradual improvement in her mood and energy levels. She began to tackle her work with renewed vigour, setting small, manageable daily goals that helped rebuild her confidence in her abilities. Her approach to work shifted from avoiding tasks to actively seeking ways to engage with her projects.

Hannah's colleagues and supervisors noticed the change as well. Her renewed participation in team meetings and her ability to meet deadlines improved dramatically. Not only did her professional life recover, but Hannah also found herself enjoying personal activities again, reconnecting with friends and family, and rediscovering hobbies that she had neglected.

By recognising the link between her procrastination and depression and seeking appropriate help, Hannah was able to turn her life around, both professionally and personally. Her story highlights the importance of addressing mental health issues head-on and demonstrates how doing so can lead to significant improvements in productivity and overall life satisfaction.

Procrastination is often a symptom rather than the root problem itself. Deep-seated psychological issues like anxiety, depression, and low self-esteem can heavily influence one's tendency to procrastinate. Understanding and addressing these underlying issues is crucial for developing more effective, long-term strategies for overcoming procrastination.

Procrastination and Depression

The link between chronic procrastination and depression is well-documented. Depression can diminish energy levels, decrease motivation, and instil a sense of worthlessness, all of which can manifest as procrastination. When tasks feel overwhelming or pointless, the immediate reaction for many is to avoid them altogether.

Addressing this aspect of procrastination involves recognising the signs of depression and seeking appropriate treatment. This could mean consulting with a mental health professional, exploring therapeutic options, and possibly considering medication. Beyond professional help, it's also beneficial to build a support network of friends, family, and peers who can offer understanding and encouragement.

Emotional Drivers

Procrastination is frequently driven by emotional factors such as anxiety about performance, fear of judgement, or the overwhelming stress that comes with high expectations. These emotions can create a paralysing fear of starting or completing tasks, as the individual may dread potential failure or criticism.

To combat these emotional triggers, it's essential to:

- Develop awareness: Recognise and name the emotions that lead to procrastination. Awareness is the first step towards change.

- Practice self-compassion: Treat yourself with the same kindness and understanding you would offer someone else in your situation. Self-compassion can mitigate the harsh self-judgement that often accompanies procrastination.

- Adopt coping strategies: Techniques such as mindfulness meditation, cognitive-behavioural therapy (CBT), and stress management exercises can help manage the anxiety and fear that fuel procrastination.

By confronting and understanding the emotional dimensions of procrastination, individuals can begin to untangle the complex web of feelings that inhibit action. This process involves both self-exploration and, often, the guidance of a professional.

Addressing the psychological roots of procrastination is not a quick fix but a transformative journey towards better mental health and productivity. By acknowledging and treating underlying mental health issues and learning to manage emotional triggers, individuals can establish a more productive behaviour pattern that extends beyond mere time management. This deeper approach allows for genuine, lasting changes in both personal and professional realms, leading to a more engaged and fulfilling life.

Types of Procrastinators

Kevin, an experienced software developer, found himself consistently avoiding tasks that involved extensive documentation or detailed reports—activities he deemed less enjoyable than the coding aspects of his job. This avoidance wasn't just a preference; it was rooted in a deep-seated fear of inadequacy and a belief that he wasn't good at these tasks, which often led to procrastination.

As deadlines loomed, Kevin's anxiety would spike, leading him to put off the tasks even further. His performance reviews began to reflect this pattern, with managers noting his exceptional coding skills but pointing out his tendency to delay less desirable tasks.

Realising that his career progression was at stake, Kevin decided it was time to confront his avoidance behaviour head-on. He started by breaking down these daunting tasks into smaller, more manageable objectives. For instance, instead of facing the overwhelming task of documenting an entire project at once, he set a goal to write one section per day.

Kevin also implemented a reward system for himself. Each time he completed a section of his documentation on schedule, he allowed himself a small reward, such as a coffee break or a short walk. These rewards not only made the process more bearable but also provided a tangible incentive to keep moving forward.

To bolster his efforts, Kevin sought feedback early in the process from peers and supervisors. This not only improved the quality of his work but also built his confidence as he realised that his fears of inadequacy were unfounded and that he was more capable than he had believed.

Over time, Kevin's approach transformed his work habits. What once felt like an insurmountable challenge became a series of small, achievable tasks. By setting realistic goals and allowing himself to build up confidence gradually, Kevin overcame his avoidance behaviour. His productivity and job satisfaction improved significantly, and his career development took a positive turn.

Kevin's story is a compelling example of how breaking down tasks and confronting avoidance head-on can lead to significant personal and professional growth. His journey from an avoider to a proactive doer illustrates the power of small, consistent steps in overcoming deep-rooted procrastination habits.

Understanding the different types of procrastinators can provide invaluable insight into why you delay tasks and how you can effectively address this behaviour. By identifying your specific type of procrastination, you can tailor strategies that are directly aligned with your personal challenges, enhancing your ability to overcome procrastination and increase productivity.

The Perfectionist

Perfectionists often procrastinate because they fear that their work won't meet their own high standards. This desire for a flawless outcome can be so overwhelming that it prevents them from starting a task at all. If you identify with this type, the key to overcoming your procrastination is to redefine your standards of success. Set realistic goals and accept that perfection is unattainable. Implement strategies like setting strict time limits for tasks to prevent endless revisions. Remember, a project that is done okay, is often better than a perfect project that is never completed.

Ryan's Perfectionism Paralysis

Ryan, a talented marketing manager at a mid-sized advertising firm, was known for his creativity and attention to detail. His campaigns were always meticulously planned, and his designs stood out for their high quality. But behind this reputation was a mounting problem—Ryan's perfectionism. It wasn't long before his relentless pursuit of flawless work began to affect his performance.

His perfectionism made even starting tasks a challenge. Ryan often spent hours fixating on minor details, tweaking and revising presentations and campaigns until the last minute. His drive for perfection delayed the start of key projects, which led to last-minute rushes, missed deadlines, and, ultimately, subpar results.

This cycle of perfectionism-fuelled procrastination reached a breaking point when Ryan was tasked with leading a high-profile marketing campaign for one of the company's biggest clients. The pressure was immense, and Ryan's perfectionist tendencies became more pronounced. He obsessed over every aspect of the campaign, from colour schemes to wording choices, unable to make decisions without doubting whether his choices were "perfect."

As the deadline loomed, Ryan's boss grew increasingly frustrated. The company had invested significant resources into this project, and the client was expecting a top-tier campaign. Yet Ryan was still stuck in the early stages of development, revising minor aspects instead of completing the campaign's core elements. His boss had already expressed concerns about Ryan's inability to meet deadlines, and now, with this high-stakes project hanging in the balance, Ryan was at risk of losing not just the client but potentially his job.

The turning point came during a tense meeting with his boss. After listening to Ryan's excuses for the delayed progress, his boss made it clear that there would be no more second chances. The campaign had to be delivered on time, even if it wasn't perfect. "I'd rather have a good campaign on time than a perfect one too late," his boss said firmly.

Realising the gravity of the situation, Ryan knew he needed to make a change. His perfectionism wasn't helping—it was destroying his career. He had to find a way to deliver results without succumbing to the paralysing fear of imperfection.

Ryan decided to take a different approach. He adopted the 80/20 Rule (Pareto Principle), which emphasises focusing on the 20% of tasks that will yield 80% of the results. This mindset helped Ryan prioritise the most impactful aspects of the campaign and let go of less critical details.

Instead of obsessing over every small element, Ryan started by identifying the key components that would make the campaign successful: the messaging, the overall concept, and the client's brand goals. By prioritising these core elements, he was able to streamline his work and move forward more efficiently. He set "good enough" standards for his work, recognising that not every detail needed to be perfect. Ryan learned to accept that achieving good results was more important than striving for unattainable perfection.

To further overcome his perfectionism, Ryan began practising incremental progress. Instead of trying to complete everything perfectly in one go, he broke the campaign into smaller stages. First, he focused on finalising the main concept and presented it to his boss for approval. Once the concept was approved, he moved on to designing the core visuals, focusing on the overall aesthetic instead of obsessing over every pixel. With each stage completed, Ryan built momentum, and the campaign started to take shape much faster than he anticipated. Only once the campaign was complete to a *good* standard did Ryan allow himself to move on to what he called the *tweaking* stage, the time to at the finishing touches, to go the last mile—his time for perfectionism.

Ryan also used a self-assessment tool to monitor his perfectionism and procrastination patterns. He asked himself critical questions to reflect on his behaviour:

- How often do I avoid starting tasks because they might not meet my high standards?

- Am I spending unnecessary time revising work that is already good enough?

- How much time am I dedicating to tasks compared to my peers?

These questions helped Ryan recognise the moments when his perfectionism was getting in the way. He started to catch himself when he was spending too much time on minor details and learned to move on without overthinking. This self-awareness became key to maintaining his progress.

In the end, Ryan completed the campaign on time. It wasn't perfect by his previous standards, but it was effective. The client was thrilled with the final product, and his boss, who had been on the verge of losing patience, praised Ryan for delivering the project on schedule. More importantly, Ryan realised that he could still produce high-quality work without being trapped by his need for perfection.

Ryan's journey taught him that perfectionism, while it may seem like a pursuit of excellence, can often lead to inaction and missed opportunities. By focusing on the most important aspects of his work and learning to accept "good enough," he was able to break free from the paralysis that had held him back.

The Dreamer

Dreamers are great at visualising success but often struggle with the practical aspects of executing their visions. They enjoy the creative process of planning but may shy away from the detailed, less glamorous work that actual execution entails. If you find yourself in this category, try breaking down your projects into smaller, actionable steps. Focus on one small task at a time, and use checklists to keep track of completed activities. This approach can make the execution as satisfying as the dreaming.

The Avoider

Avoiders typically procrastinate due to a fear of failure or even a fear of success. They might feel that by not completing a task, they can avoid dealing with potential negative outcomes. If this resonates with you, confront the fears that are holding you back. Practice exposure by gradually taking on slightly challenging tasks and building up your confidence with each small success. Also, seeking feedback early and often is important to reduce the fear associated with final outcomes.

The Crisis-Maker

Crisis-makers thrive on the adrenaline rush that comes with last-minute work. They may believe they perform best under pressure, but this often leads to stress and burnout. If you are a crisis-maker, start by gradually shifting your deadlines forward. Give yourself earlier "fake" deadlines to avoid the rush, and gradually increase the amount of time you allow for each task. Learn to find satisfaction in the peace that comes with completing work ahead of time, rather than during a last-minute panic.

By identifying which type of procrastinator you are—the Perfectionist, the Dreamer, the Avoider, or the Crisis-Maker—you can implement targeted strategies that address the root causes of your procrastination. This tailored approach not only makes the process of overcoming procrastination more manageable but also more effective, leading to long-term improvements in productivity and satisfaction in your work. The journey to overcoming procrastination begins with self-awareness and is sustained by the strategic application of personalised, effective techniques.

The Overwhelmed Mind: Addressing Procrastination in Individuals with ADHD

Sophia's Struggle with ADHD

Sophia, a talented graphic designer, had always been praised for her creativity and artistic vision. However, behind the scenes, she struggled with chronic procrastination. Diagnosed with ADHD in her teens, Sophia found it difficult to manage the multiple deadlines that came with her work. She excelled at the design elements of her job but frequently delayed administrative tasks such as client communications and project documentation.

Sophia's procrastination wasn't just a matter of disinterest; it was rooted in her ADHD symptoms, which made organising and prioritising tasks incredibly challenging. Instead of tackling her growing to-do list, she often jumped between projects or got distracted by new ideas, leaving a trail of unfinished work. This disorganisation resulted in missed deadlines, frustrated clients, and a growing sense of stress and overwhelm.

Crisis Point:

Sophia reached a breaking point when she missed the deadline for a major project, costing her the chance to work with a prestigious client. Her manager warned that her inability to meet deadlines could jeopardise her position at the company. Realising her career was at risk, Sophia knew she needed to confront her procrastination head-on.

Advanced Strategy:

Sophia adopted the Pomodoro Technique, a time management method where she worked in short, focused bursts of 25 minutes, followed by 5-minute breaks. This structure gave her the mental space to focus without feeling overwhelmed. She combined this technique with mind mapping, visually organising her projects into smaller, manageable tasks, which allowed her to see the full scope of her work and prioritise accordingly.

Self-Assessment Tool:

Sophia also used a self-assessment tool to track her procrastination patterns, asking herself questions like:

- Do I frequently start multiple tasks but struggle to complete them?

- Do I find it difficult to prioritise tasks?

- How often do I feel overwhelmed by the number of tasks I need to complete?

This self-awareness helped her recognise how her ADHD symptoms contributed to her procrastination. By breaking tasks into smaller steps and scheduling work in short bursts, Sophia transformed her workflow and met her deadlines consistently.

Outcome:

Sophia's new approach improved her productivity significantly. By acknowledging her ADHD and adopting tailored strategies, she was able to manage her workload more effectively. Her manager noticed the improvement, and Sophia regained confidence in her ability to balance creativity with structure.

The Gentle Resilience: Overcoming Procrastination Due to Depression

Tom's Battle with Depression

Tom, a gifted writer, had always dreamed of completing a novel, but his struggle with depression made it nearly impossible to begin, let alone finish, any major project. Depression drained him of energy and motivation, leaving him feeling stuck and overwhelmed by even the simplest tasks. The idea of writing, which once excited him, now filled him with dread. His procrastination deepened his feelings of guilt and failure, leading to a vicious cycle of avoidance.

Crisis Point:

Tom's procrastination reached a critical point when his publisher issued a firm deadline for his next book. He had been granted multiple extensions, but now he risked losing his contract entirely if he didn't deliver. Tom knew he needed to break the cycle of avoidance before his career was permanently derailed.

Advanced Strategy:

Tom turned to Behavioural Activation Therapy (BAT), a form of therapy that encourages individuals to engage in meaningful activities to combat depression. He started small—setting a goal to write for just 10 minutes a day. This manageable task helped him push past the overwhelming nature of writing a full chapter. As he completed these small goals, he gradually increased the time spent writing.

Tom also incorporated gratitude journaling into his routine. By focusing on positive aspects of his life, he was able to shift his mindset away from negative thoughts and boost his mood, which in turn reduced his procrastination.

Self-Assessment Tool:

Tom used a self-assessment tool to monitor his mood and energy levels daily. His self-assessment questions included:

- How motivated do I feel today on a scale of 1-10?

- How much interest do I have in my daily activities?

- Have I experienced feelings of hopelessness or worthlessness today?

By tracking his emotional state, Tom was able to see the connection between his mood and his procrastination habits. When he noticed his mood slipping, he would adjust his routine to focus on smaller, more achievable goals.

Outcome:

Tom's gradual approach led to a breakthrough. By writing just a little each day, he eventually completed his manuscript, and the publisher was pleased with the quality of his work. More importantly, Tom learned to manage his depression by setting small, achievable goals and focusing on positive aspects of his life. His self-confidence grew, and the cycle of procrastination began to break.

The Cautious Striver: Dealing with Anxiety-Induced Procrastination

Lisa's Anxiety and Procrastination Cycle

Lisa, a bright and ambitious college student, was known for her academic excellence. However, beneath her achievements was a constant battle with anxiety, particularly when it came to academic performance. Every time she had an assignment or exam, her fear of failure became so intense that she would procrastinate, avoiding the work altogether. The irony was that the more she delayed, the more her anxiety grew, trapping her in a cycle of stress and avoidance.

In her final year, Lisa's procrastination nearly cost her a passing grade in a critical course. She delayed studying for her final exams, paralysed by the fear that no amount of preparation would be enough. As the exam date approached, Lisa's anxiety spiked, and she considered dropping the class altogether to avoid the shame of failing.

Lisa sought help through Cognitive Behavioural Therapy (CBT), where she learned to challenge and reframe her negative thought patterns. Instead of thinking, "If I don't get an A, I'm a failure," she replaced these thoughts with, "Doing my best is enough." She also practised Exposure Therapy, gradually exposing herself to tasks that provoked anxiety, such as completing small assignments first, and eventually building up to larger tasks like final exams.

To better understand her anxiety triggers, Lisa used a self-assessment tool with questions like:

- What thoughts arise when I think about starting a task?

- On a scale of 1-10, how intense is my fear of failure?

- How often do I avoid tasks due to anxiety?

By identifying the moments when her anxiety was highest, Lisa could apply CBT techniques more effectively, catching herself before her procrastination spiralled out of control.

With these strategies in place, Lisa was able to complete her final exams on time and with far less anxiety than before. She didn't achieve a perfect grade, but she passed with flying colours and felt proud of her effort. Lisa learned that her worth wasn't tied to her academic performance and that confronting her anxiety, rather than avoiding it, was the key to breaking the procrastination cycle.

Cultural and Personal Differences

Amita, originally from a South Asian background where meticulous care and thorough planning were valued over speedy execution, found herself struggling when she took a job at a dynamic startup in the heart of Silicon Valley. The fast-paced environment, where quick decisions and rapid task completion were the norms, starkly contrasted with the deliberate pace she was accustomed to.

In her first few months, Amita often felt rushed and uncomfortable with the expectation of immediate results, fearing that the quality of her work would suffer. Her natural inclination to reflect deeply on problems and explore all possible outcomes before taking action led to procrastination in a setting where such thoroughness was often seen as hesitation or inefficiency.

Recognising that she needed to adapt to thrive in her new role, Amita sought a middle ground that respected her cultural approach to work while meeting the demands of her new environment. She started by identifying which tasks required swift decisions and which benefited from a more detailed exploration. This allowed her to allocate her time more effectively, applying her depth of thought to complex strategic decisions that could have a longer-term impact, while speeding up on more routine or time-sensitive tasks.

To further integrate into her workplace, Amita adopted several time-management techniques, such as the Pomodoro Technique, to keep herself on track with more immediate deadlines. She also began scheduling brief daily review sessions with her team, which allowed her to quickly gather input and make informed decisions.

As Amita became more comfortable with this blended approach, her unique capability to combine thorough analysis with efficiency became her strength. Her team began to value her ability to bring depth to strategic projects while also respecting the quick pace of the startup environment.

Amita's story showcases how understanding and integrating different cultural approaches to work can enhance rather than hinder productivity. Her ability to adapt while staying true to her thorough nature not only helped her overcome procrastination but also turned her into a pivotal member of her team, bridging the gap between careful deliberation and the necessity for speed.

Recognising the impact of cultural backgrounds and personal upbringings is crucial for a comprehensive understanding of procrastination behaviours. These factors can shape how individuals approach work and productivity, often in ways that are deeply ingrained and subconscious. By examining these influences, you can gain insights that not only enhance personal understanding but also improve interactions and productivity within diverse teams.

Cultural Influences

Cultural norms play a significant role in defining what is considered productive behaviour. In some cultures, meticulous care and attention to detail are valued above speed and efficiency. This methodical approach can sometimes be misinterpreted as procrastination by those from cultures that prioritise quick results and time efficiency. For instance, in many Western business environments, rapid task completion is often celebrated, whereas in many parts of Asia, the emphasis might be on deliberation and consensus, which takes longer.

Recognising these differences is essential not only for personal productivity but also for working effectively in multicultural settings. It requires an understanding that different cultures bring different strengths to the table, and what might initially appear as procrastination could actually be a careful, thoughtful approach to problem-solving.

Personal Upbringing

The environment in which a person is raised can also significantly influence their work habits. Individuals who grew up in environments where they were frequently criticised might develop procrastination as a defensive mechanism. This behaviour can be a way to avoid criticism or negative feedback, as not completing a task means not having to present it for potential scrutiny.

To overcome procrastination influenced by upbringing, it is helpful to work on building self-confidence and learning to separate past experiences from current realities. Techniques such as cognitive-behavioural therapy (CBT) can be effective in addressing these deep-seated fears and reshaping one's approach to work and productivity.

Managing Expectations and Developing Customised Approaches

Understanding the cultural and personal roots of procrastination can help manage expectations and develop customised strategies that enhance productivity. For individuals, this means taking the time to reflect on what influences their work habits and actively working to create an approach that respects their background while pushing them towards greater efficiency.

For teams, it involves fostering an environment where diverse work styles are recognised and valued. This could mean adjusting project timelines to accommodate different paces of work or creating a more supportive feedback system that helps all team members feel valued and understood.

Acknowledging and understanding the impact of cultural and personal differences in procrastination behaviours is not just about improving individual productivity; it's about creating more harmonious and effective work environments. By embracing these differences, individuals and teams can foster a deeper understanding and respect for varied work styles, ultimately leading to more thoughtful, inclusive, and productive ways of working.

There's A Lot To It

In this chapter, we've explored the multifaceted nature of procrastination, delving deep into the underlying issues that often precipitate this behaviour. Addressing these root causes is not merely about improving productivity; it's about fostering a deeper understanding of our psychological makeup and the social influences that shape our actions.

Procrastination is often symptomatic of deeper psychological issues such as depression and anxiety, which can distort our perception of tasks and magnify the fear of beginning them. Recognising these emotional drivers is crucial; it is the first step towards healing and developing more constructive approaches to managing our responsibilities. Moreover, identifying the specific type of procrastinator you are can help tailor interventions that are much more effective, allowing personalised strategies to take shape.

Cultural and personal differences also play significant roles in how procrastination manifests. What might be considered procrastination in one cultural context could be seen as careful deliberation in another. Acknowledging and respecting these differences is essential for managing expectations and fostering environments where diverse work styles are appreciated and nurtured.

Finally, the journey towards overcoming procrastination is continuous and dynamic. It requires an openness to adapt and refine strategies as you gain more insight into your personal triggers and the broader cultural factors at play. The goal is not to eradicate procrastination entirely but to understand it well enough to manage it effectively. By doing so, we not only enhance our own productivity and well-being but also contribute to a more compassionate and accommodating atmosphere for others facing similar challenges.

This comprehensive approach to understanding and addressing procrastination paves the way for more effective personal and professional growth, enabling us to take more control over our actions and, ultimately, our lives.

Overcoming Specific Fears

Fear is a powerful motivator that can either spur us to action or paralyse us into inaction. In the context of procrastination, fear often serves as a barrier that prevents us from moving forward with our goals. This chapter addresses how to confront and overcome specific common fears that contribute to procrastination, helping you to embrace challenges and uncertainties with confidence.

Fear of Change

Sarah had been a primary school teacher for over a decade, cherished by pupils and respected by her colleagues. However, despite her success, she felt an increasing pull towards a different passion—interior design. The idea of changing careers was daunting; teaching was all she knew, and the thought of starting from scratch in a completely different field filled her with anxiety.

Her fear of change kept her from pursuing her new interest for years. She worried about the financial implications, the steep learning curve, and, most of all, the possibility of failure in a field where she had no formal experience. These fears led her to procrastinate on making any real decisions, trapping her in a state of inaction and dissatisfaction.

The turning point came when Sarah attended a weekend workshop on interior design, which was intended to explore her interests. The experience was transformative. Being actively engaged in design work, even briefly, reignited her passion and gave her a glimpse of the joy and fulfilment she had been missing.

Motivated by this experience, Sarah began taking small steps towards her new career. She enrolled in evening classes in interior design, gradually building her skills and confidence. As she learned more about the industry, her fear of change diminished. She started taking on small freelance projects, which not only expanded her portfolio but also her belief in her ability to succeed in this new world.

Eventually, Sarah felt prepared to make a complete transition. She resigned from her teaching position and launched her own interior design business. The change was not without its challenges, but with each project, her reputation grew. She discovered a deep satisfaction in helping transform people's living spaces, which was markedly different from her previous career but fulfilling in new and exciting ways.

Sarah's journey from a seasoned teacher to a successful interior designer is a powerful testament to the rewards of embracing change. By confronting her fear of the unknown and taking incremental steps towards her passion, she was able to not only achieve a successful career shift but also find greater personal fulfilment and happiness. Her story illustrates that embracing change, despite its initial fears, can lead to discovering new paths and opportunities that align more closely with one's passions and aspirations.

Change is inevitable in both personal and professional life, yet the uncertainty associated with change can often be intimidating.

- Understanding Change: Recognise that change is often a sign of progress and growth. Reframe your perspective to view change as an opportunity to learn and develop new skills.

- Small Steps: Start with small changes to build your confidence. Gradual adjustments can help you manage the anxiety associated with larger shifts in your routine or work environment.

- Support System: When facing significant changes, lean on a support system of friends, family, or colleagues who can provide encouragement and perspective.

Fear of Others' Judgements

Mark, a young and aspiring biotechnologist, had been working on a revolutionary project that could potentially change the way certain diseases are diagnosed. Despite the innovative nature of his work, Mark was held back by a deep-seated fear of public criticism. This fear stemmed from an earlier career incident in which he received harsh feedback during a team meeting, which left him doubting his abilities and value as a researcher.

As his project neared completion, Mark was presented with the opportunity to showcase his findings at a prestigious international biotechnology conference. The thought of presenting his research to a large audience of esteemed peers was daunting. He was terrified of being judged, criticised, or dismissed, and this fear led him to consider declining the invitation to speak.

However, with encouragement from his mentor, Mark decided to face his fears. He recognised that this presentation could be a pivotal moment for both his personal growth and the success of his project. To prepare, he spent weeks refining his presentation, conducting additional experiments to ensure his data was robust, and practising his speaking skills in front of supportive colleagues to build his confidence.

The day of the conference arrived, and despite his nerves, Mark delivered his presentation with more poise and clarity than he had thought possible. To his surprise, the feedback was overwhelmingly positive. Several leading researchers in the field expressed interest in his work, offering constructive and encouraging comments. One esteemed professor from another country approached him with a proposal for collaboration, seeing potential applications of Mark's work in her own research.

This experience marked a significant turning point for Mark. The successful presentation not only alleviated his fear of public criticism but also opened doors to several exciting opportunities for professional collaboration and development. He returned from the conference with a renewed sense of confidence in his abilities and a realisation that constructive feedback, even when critical, was a valuable tool for growth and improvement.

Mark's story illustrates how confronting a fear of judgement and taking a risk by stepping into the spotlight can lead to unexpected professional achievements and personal development. His breakthrough at the conference not only advanced his career but also transformed his approach to future challenges, which he now views as opportunities to learn and excel.

Worrying about what others think can be a significant hindrance to taking action, especially when it comes to creative or public endeavours.

- Self-Validation: Focus on building self-validation rather than seeking external approval. Recognise your accomplishments and value your own opinion of your work.

- Constructive Feedback: Learn to differentiate between constructive criticism and mere opinion. Use constructive feedback to improve, while ignoring unhelpful negativity.

- Confidence Building: Regularly engage in activities that build your self-confidence. This could be through public speaking, sharing your work with trusted peers, or pursuing further education in your field.

Fear of Unknown Outcomes

Olivia had always dreamed of opening her own bakery. With a background in culinary arts and several years of experience in high-end restaurants, she felt prepared in terms of skills but was haunted by the fear of the unknown outcomes of starting her own business. The food industry is notoriously challenging, with high competition and a significant risk of failure, which exacerbated her anxieties about taking the leap.

Her procrastination to start her business stemmed from a deep-seated fear of failing and losing her investment, not to mention the potential public embarrassment if her venture didn't succeed. These fears kept Olivia from pursuing her dream for years, until a mentor challenged her perspective during a casual conversation. The mentor advised Olivia to focus not on the fear of failure, but on the potential for learning and growth, regardless of the outcome.

Motivated by this new mindset, Olivia decided to approach her bakery venture as an educational journey rather than a win-or-lose scenario. She started small, initially launching her business online to minimise overhead costs. She viewed every aspect of setting up her business—from crafting her menu and sourcing ingredients to marketing and customer service—as part of a continuous learning process.

Each setback became a lesson instead of a mark of failure. For instance, when a particular product didn't sell as expected, Olivia used it as an opportunity to engage with her customers and gain insights into their preferences, which she then used to refine her offerings. This iterative approach helped Olivia gradually build a loyal customer base.

Her commitment to learning paid off. As her understanding of the business grew, so did her confidence. Within a year, Olivia's online bakery was thriving, prompting her to open a small physical storefront. The bakery quickly became a local favourite, known for its innovative flavours and warm, inviting atmosphere.

Olivia's success wasn't just in her thriving business but in overcoming her fear of the unknown. By shifting her focus to learning and growth, she was able to navigate the uncertainties of entrepreneurship with resilience and adaptability. Her bakery not only fulfilled her dream but also became a testament to the value of embracing the unknown as an opportunity for personal and professional development.

The uncertainty of outcomes can lead to procrastination, especially when the stakes are high.

- Scenario Planning: Practice scenario planning, where you visualise various outcomes and plan your responses. This can reduce the fear associated with unknown results.

- Mindfulness and Acceptance: Develop mindfulness practices that focus on living in the present rather than worrying about future outcomes. Accept that you cannot control everything and focus on exerting influence where you can.

- Incremental Learning: Embrace a learning mindset where every outcome, whether success or failure, is seen as an opportunity to learn and improve. This approach reduces the pressure to achieve perfection and mitigates the fear of failure.

By understanding and addressing the specific fears that fuel procrastination, you can unlock your potential and move forward with greater purpose and confidence. Each section in this chapter provides strategies not just for coping with fear, but for transforming it into a force that drives rather than deters personal and professional development.

Case Studies and Real-Life Success Stories

This chapter presents a selection of inspiring case studies from various fields, illustrating how individuals overcame procrastination through strategic changes in behaviour, mindset, and lifestyle. Each story provides insights and lessons that can motivate and guide you to tackle your own procrastination challenges.

Emily's Tech Triumph

Emily's journey as a software developer at an innovative tech startup is a story of personal and professional transformation. With a background steeped in creativity and innovation—thanks to a family that celebrated technological curiosity—Emily developed a passion for coding from a young age. This environment nurtured her aspirations to not just participate in the tech world but to lead and innovate within it.

Despite her clear talent and passion, Emily encountered significant hurdles. The daunting nature of the task ahead often overshadowed her deep-seated desire to create groundbreaking software features. The intensity of focus required for coding, combined with high self-imposed expectations, led Emily to regularly procrastinate. She found herself routinely shifting focus to less demanding tasks, avoiding the intricate coding work that required her full concentration and creative energy.

The underlying cause of Emily's procrastination was a mix of fear of underperforming and the overwhelming pressure she placed on herself to excel. These pressures made starting the most challenging parts of her work feel insurmountable at times.

Determined to break this cycle and not let procrastination define her career, Emily implemented a structured approach to her workday. She adopted the Pomodoro Technique, which involves working in focused 25-minute bursts followed by short breaks. This method allowed her to manage her focus and energy more effectively, making daunting tasks feel more manageable and less intimidating. Additionally, Emily began using a digital tool to block social media and other distractions, ensuring her work periods were free from interruptions.

This new approach revolutionised Emily's productivity. Structured intervals of concentrated work allowed her to dive deep into her tasks without the mental burden of fearing the hours ahead. The regular, short breaks rejuvenated her focus and staved off fatigue, allowing her to maintain high performance throughout the day.

Within just a few months, Emily's enhanced productivity was evident. She began delivering complex software features faster and with greater efficiency. Her remarkable performance led to a well-deserved promotion to Lead Developer, acknowledging her leadership skills and consistent delivery of high-quality work. This role was a significant milestone towards realising her long-term career goals and affirmed her potential to lead and innovate in the tech industry.

Emily's story is a powerful testament to the effectiveness of the Pomodoro Technique in overcoming procrastination, particularly for tasks requiring deep thought and concentration. Her experience illustrates that with the right strategies, even the most daunting tasks can be approached effectively.

For anyone struggling with procrastination, especially on complex projects, integrating structured time management techniques like the Pomodoro can be transformative. It not only boosts productivity but also enhances job satisfaction and fosters career advancement, turning potential stumbling blocks into stepping stones for success. Emily's journey from procrastination to productivity serves as an inspiring example of how adopting practical, focused work strategies can lead to significant personal and professional achievements.

Jack's Journey to Becoming an Author

Jack, a passionate yet intermittently motivated writer, had always harboured the dream of penning a novel that could captivate readers and perhaps even grace the bestseller lists. Growing up in a modest family where storytelling was the heart of evening gatherings, Jack's love for writing was kindled by his grandmother's intricate tales and his father's wide collection of classic literature. These influences filled him with a desire to one day see his own words in print, inspiring others as he had been inspired.

However, despite his aspirations and a mind brimming with ideas, Jack found himself ensnared by procrastination. He believed that perfect conditions—quiet, uninterrupted hours and bursts of inspiration—were necessary to begin writing. Consequently, years slipped by with Jack writing only sporadically, never quite managing to establish a consistent writing habit.

Realising that waiting for the "perfect moment" was a futile endeavour keeping him from his goals, Jack decided it was time for a change. He committed to a seemingly modest but significant daily goal: writing at least 500 words, regardless of his inspiration level or the immediate quality of his work.

To bolster this new commitment, Jack joined a local writing group. This wasn't just any group but a community of fellow aspiring writers who met weekly to share progress and provide constructive feedback. The group's structured environment offered not only regular accountability but also a platform for receiving and giving critiques, which was instrumental in refining his craft.

Jack's strategy of setting manageable daily word counts proved transformative. The goal of 500 words a day was enough to keep him engaged without feeling overwhelmed. This newfound consistency allowed him to make steady progress, and the routine helped him overcome the initial resistance he faced each day. The regular interaction with his writing group became a cornerstone of his progress, offering milestones to celebrate his achievements and insights to propel him further.

Within eight months, a period filled with both challenges and triumphs, Jack completed his manuscript. Through this process, he learned that success in large projects doesn't come from waiting for grand bursts of inspiration but from small, consistent efforts that accumulate over time. The daily discipline of writing 500 words became not just a practice but a meditative ritual that steadily brought his dream into reality.

Additionally, the camaraderie and accountability provided by his writing group were critical. They offered not just encouragement but crucial feedback that significantly improved his writing.

For anyone struggling with procrastination, particularly on large projects, Jack's story illuminates a path forward. Setting small, achievable daily goals can lead to significant accomplishments. Furthermore, engaging with a supportive community, whether it's a writing group, a study circle, or a professional network, can provide the necessary encouragement and accountability to keep progressing. By embracing these strategies, you might find that you not only complete your projects but also enhance the quality and enjoyment of your work. Like Jack, adopting these approaches can transform a stagnant aspiration into a dynamic and fulfilling journey to success.

Linda's Boutique Breakthrough

Linda's lifelong passion for fashion drove her dream of owning a boutique in the bustling town centre shopping area. Growing up in a small town, she was fascinated by the transformative power of clothing and envisioned herself creating a space that could offer unique fashion experiences to others. Her boutique was more than a business; it was a personal statement, a manifestation of her creativity and entrepreneurial spirit.

Despite her deep commitment and passion, Linda found herself struggling with the day-to-day management of her boutique. She excelled in the creative aspects of her business, such as curating collections and designing store layouts, but procrastinated on the less glamorous yet critical tasks like inventory management and financial planning. Her casual approach to these crucial areas often led to overstocked items and missed opportunities for seasonal promotions, which directly impacted her bottom line.

Realising that her procrastination was jeopardising the sustainability of her dream, Linda decided to make a pivotal change. She turned to technology, adopting a comprehensive business management app specifically designed for small retail businesses. This tool was a game-changer for Linda; it seamlessly integrated inventory tracking with sales data, providing real-time insights that were previously obscured by her ad-hoc management style.

Another strategic move was introducing clear, measurable quarterly goals. Linda focused on increasing foot traffic, boosting online sales, and optimising inventory turnover. The business management app not only simplified these tasks but also provided actionable insights that allowed Linda to adjust her strategies in real time based on current trends and customer feedback.

With these tools and a renewed focus on efficiency, Linda transformed her approach to business management. She could now make informed purchasing decisions, effectively reducing waste and avoiding overstock. Her stock became more aligned with customer demand, and her marketing efforts became more targeted and effective.

Within a year of implementing these technological and strategic changes, Linda's boutique saw a significant increase in profitability. This success was a direct result of better inventory control and strategic marketing, fueled by the data and insights provided by her new business management system.

Linda's journey is a testament to the power of embracing technology to overcome procrastination and enhance business efficiency. Her story illustrates that while passion and creativity are vital, the successful realisation of a dream also requires attention to the mundane yet critical aspects of business. For entrepreneurs and business owners, Linda's experience underscores the importance of leveraging the right tools to transform overwhelming tasks into manageable ones, allowing them to focus more on growth and customer engagement.

Her story is a powerful reminder that with the right tools and a strategic approach, even the most daunting challenges can be transformed into opportunities for growth and success. Linda not only maintained her boutique's unique character but also ensured its profitability and sustainability, allowing her to continue pursuing her passion for fashion while running a successful business.

Sam's Academic Ascent

Sam, a PhD student in environmental science, was deeply passionate about his research on sustainable urban planning. Raised in a community where environmental conservation was a communal responsibility, Sam grew up with a profound respect for nature and a desire to make a significant impact through his work. This passion led him to pursue advanced studies with aspirations of transforming urban environments through sustainable practices.

Despite his commitment and deep interest in his field, Sam struggled with a significant hurdle: procrastination. The root of his procrastination was not laziness but overwhelming fear. The magnitude of his dissertation project and the high expectations he set for himself created a paralysing fear of failure. This fear was compounded by his anticipation of harsh criticism from a highly esteemed advisory committee, whose approval he desperately sought.

This anxiety manifested in Sam delaying work on his dissertation, busying himself with less important tasks to avoid directly facing his main project. As deadlines approached, the anxiety and procrastination cycle intensified, threatening to derail his academic goals.

Realising that this pattern could jeopardise his PhD, Sam decided to confront his fear head-on by altering his approach to his dissertation work. Instead of isolating himself and attempting to craft perfect, fully-formed chapters in one go, he chose to engage more proactively with his advisor.

Sam initiated regular bi-weekly meetings with his advisor, a strategy that allowed him to tackle his dissertation in smaller, more manageable sections. This approach not only made the task seem less daunting but also provided him with continuous feedback, preventing him from veering off track. Each session became a stepping stone, gradually building his confidence and demystifying the expectations of his committee.

These feedback sessions proved invaluable. They not only clarified his thoughts and refined his arguments but also transformed his advisory relationship from one of apprehension to one of mentorship and support. The iterative feedback process alleviated his anxiety, kept him accountable, and ensured his dissertation was a product of both his innovation and scholarly guidance.

By the time Sam was ready to defend his dissertation, he had gained something invaluable—confidence in the rigour and validity of his work, forged through the fires of regular critique and incremental improvement. He successfully defended his dissertation and earned his PhD with commendations from the very committee he had once feared.

Sam's journey underscores the power of breaking large, intimidating tasks into smaller, manageable parts and the critical role of seeking early and ongoing feedback. For those facing daunting projects, adopting Sam's strategy of regular check-ins and iterative feedback can ease anxieties, enhance the quality of work, and transform a solitary struggle into a collaborative success. This approach not only addresses the root causes of procrastination but also turns a formidable challenge into a series of achievable milestones.

It's Real Life

The examples in this chapter illustrate the powerful impact of addressing procrastination with specific strategies tailored to individual needs and circumstances. By drawing inspiration from these success stories, you can find practical methods and motivation to overcome your own hurdles related to procrastination. Each story not only showcases the triumphs of individuals across various fields but also serves as a beacon of what can be accomplished when you commit to change.

Moving Forward with Momentum

As we reach the conclusion of this journey, it's essential to reflect on the insights and strategies we've explored to overcome procrastination. This book has equipped you with an understanding of the psychological barriers that foster procrastination, practical techniques to combat it, and real-life stories of individuals who have successfully transformed their habits and, consequently, their lives.

We started by identifying the psychological roots of procrastination, such as fear of failure and fear of success, which can paralyse action. We then moved on to practical strategies like setting small goals, organising tasks, and managing time effectively to build a routine that fosters productivity. We delved into advanced techniques such as using technology to aid productivity, creating accountability, and setting up reward systems to sustain motivation. We also discussed the importance of habit-building and how establishing and maintaining productive habits can lead to long-term success. Lastly, we explored special topics and case studies that highlighted individual journeys and the diverse approaches people have taken to overcome procrastination in various fields.

Now, armed with knowledge and tools, you stand at the threshold of change. Remember, overcoming procrastination is not about perfection; it's about progression. It's about making incremental improvements each day that will compound over time to yield significant results. The strategies outlined in this book are not merely theoretical; they are practical, tested, and transformative. Embrace them, adapt them to your context, and commit to making a change.

As the author of this book and someone who has ventured through the highs and lows of multiple business endeavours, I've faced my fair share of procrastination, stemming from a myriad of sources. My journey through procrastination has been as varied as the businesses I've started, each presenting its unique set of challenges and learning opportunities.

In the early days of my entrepreneurial career, I realised that procrastination was not merely a bad habit but a complex reaction to underlying fears and discomforts. For instance, when I launched my first technology startup, I found myself delaying tasks that required technical skills which were outside my comfort zone. I was adept at conceptual thinking and business strategy but less so in the nitty-gritty of software development. The fear of engaging deeply in areas where I lacked expertise led to procrastination.

The breakthrough came when I began applying one of the strategies I later detailed in this book: taking baby steps. I broke down overwhelming projects into smaller, manageable tasks, each designed to slowly build my competence and confidence. Over time, as my skills improved, so did my willingness to tackle challenging projects head-on.

However, my battle with procrastination wasn't always tied to professional inadequacies. During a particularly tumultuous period in my personal life, involving a family health crisis, I noticed my productivity plummeting once again. This time, the emotional turmoil was seeping into my work, making it difficult to maintain focus and momentum. Recognising this, I leaned on another strategy discussed in this book: seeking community support and focusing on emotional well-being. I joined support groups and engaged more openly with my peers about my struggles, which significantly alleviated the mental burden I was carrying.

Each phase of my life required a different approach to overcome procrastination. What worked once did not necessarily work again under different circumstances. This was a pivotal realisation for me—one that I hope resonates with you. The strategies outlined in this book are tools, and like any tool, their effectiveness depends on the context in which they are used.

Remember that overcoming procrastination is not about finding a one-size-fits-all solution. It's about understanding the underlying causes of your procrastination in each situation and applying the right strategies to address them. It's about being flexible and adaptive, willing to try different approaches, and being forgiving of yourself when one method doesn't fit. Just as I have navigated through my unique challenges by adapting and learning, I encourage you to approach your procrastination with a similar mindset of exploration and adaptation.

As we conclude this journey together, think of this book not just as a guide but as a companion in your ongoing battle against procrastination. Embrace the strategies, experiment with them, and find what works best for you in your current circumstances. With persistence and the right tools, you can transform procrastination from a roadblock into a pathway to success.

Change is a journey that doesn't have to be walked alone. I invite you to join our community of like-minded individuals who are all committed to beating procrastination and achieving their fullest potential. In this community, you'll find support, motivation, and perhaps even inspiration from the stories of others who are on the same path as you.

Additionally, consider exploring follow-up resources such as workshops, webinars, and further readings to deepen your understanding and refine your skills. Continuous learning is key to continuous improvement.

As you close this book, remember that every page you've read is a step towards a more productive and fulfilled life. The path to overcoming procrastination is laid out before you. Take the first step, then another, and keep going. Progress, no matter how small initially, is progress nonetheless.

I encourage you to start today. Choose one strategy from this book and implement it. Then, build on that. Momentum will grow, and soon, you'll look back and marvel not just at how far you've come, but at how your journey has inspired others to embark on their own.

Together, let's move forward from procrastination to action, from dreams to reality. Let this book not just be a guide but a catalyst for transformation. It's time to begin!

For more resources, visit www.chrisball.com

* 9 7 8 1 9 1 5 4 4 9 8 4 9 *